HOW TO GET A BETTER JOB
IN MANAGEMENT

HOW TO GET A BETTER JOB IN MANAGEMENT

Ian MacHorton

Mercury House London

First published 1971

ISBN 0 220 66830 2

This book has been set in 10 on 11 pt Times and printed by The Camelot Press Ltd, London and Southampton for the publishers Business Books Limited (registered office: 180 Fleet Street, London, E.C.4) publishing offices: Mercury House, Waterloo Road, London, S.E.1

Made and printed in Great Britain

CONTENTS

PREFACE

If you ask ten different people how to get a job you are certain to get ten different answers. It is the job hunter's task to create the most suitable mix of those answers to ensure his personal success. This book presents a distillation of possible answers to help you formulate your own tactics within the new concept of a personal marketing campaign.

Acknowledgements

I am indebted to my colleagues of 'Operation Bowler', Peter Lewis-Bizley and Charles Lamb for their contribution to this work, and to Mr J. G. Smith, Managing Director of Management Selection Limited, for making information and material available to me.

CHAPTER ONE

INTRODUCING THE PROBLEM

Gone are the days when a young man joined a company, worked hard for forty years, felt secure in a senior position, and was gently pensioned off in his early sixties. The 1970s are seeing the emergence of a new pattern of executive employment—the two career structure. The complexities of modern management require that the senior man has, in addition to the great experience he has gained over the years, a sound knowledge of all aspects of management. He requires wide horizons gained through experience of other organisations, products and markets, and as much detail as possible of the aids to management which are vital for him to do his job effectively. Thus, a career in management today must be *planned* with the greatest care:

> The analysis of the skills required by the 'top man', at the present time, and in ten year's time.
>
> The selection of the professional route to the top, e.g. accountancy, marketing, engineering, and then on to general management.
>
> The personal training required to attain the skills necessary to reach those rungs of the ladder which matter.

Once the objectives have been set and the approximate route decided, training oneself to be fitted for the senior jobs becomes important.

In our present economic climate the need to reduce operating overheads and increase productivity has forced companies to merge, to take over other firms, and to examine critically the contribution which every individual makes to the profits of the organisation. Thus, if they are to stay in business (that is to say, continue to make a satisfactory profit), companies must devise their own methods of evaluating the contribution of every employee. This I call the *individual contribution factor*. Every job can be analysed and a set of criteria drawn up to determine a man's contribution to profitability. Some jobs are very easy to evaluate, for example that of a salesman. His contribution factor could be calculated as follows:

Salary + pension costs Cost of car, running, etc. Share of promotion overheads Share of administrative overheads (rent, rates, heat, light, office space, telephone, secretarial services), taxes, contributions, etc. Profit required on sales Cost of sales, etc.	= His minimum sales target, i.e. his break-even point

Hence, the salesman who achieves this minimum figure is only just paying his way, and obviously comes under the microscope. He must increase his contribution factor or expect the consequences.

The point is that every employee must contribute to profitability for the company to stay in business, and it is in the individual's own interest to examine and appraise his own contribution, and then do something about improving it.

So many executives sit complacently in their offices doing the job efficiently, yet in a state of false security. They have not realised their jobs are changing. They are growing, expanding, making greater demands upon them, their ability, their enthusiasm, their time. Suddenly the job is too big for them, because they have made no effort to grow larger with the job. Then the time comes—that moment which may come to anyone else but never to him—when the boss says (beautifully packaged): 'Sorry, Charlie! It's the parting of the ways. We have got to cut back . . . blessing in disguise . . . you'll have no trouble . . . may be *me* next . . . six months' pay . . . start looking right away . . . end of the month . . . car keys . . . cards . . . GOOD LUCK and, by the way, Happy Fiftieth Birthday.'

The 'patient' is in a state of shock. It is to help him recover, to come out fighting and to help him start again that this book has been written.

The problem you face

A conservative estimate of the number of executives unemployed at this time is 70,000. Very few of them are specialists in high demand; the vast majority are average, run-of-the-mill managers at the middle level. They come from all sizes of companies, from all types of industry, from all varieties of background. They are salesmen, marketing men, ad. men, accountants, administrators, production men and any other profession you may like to mention. Apart from a small percentage, they are all capable, enthusiastic and willing. They are all in varying degrees of mental shock, they are financially worried, and they have a feeling of having failed somewhere along the line. They are job-hungry.

Add to this figure executive material (officers, warrant officers and senior NCOs) thrown on to the market every year by the armed forces, senior men from the Civil Service, and those executives (estimated at 30 per cent of those earning over £3000 a year) who are looking for something better than their present job, and one sees the enormity of the competition which you face. Couple with this the fact that the original cause of the unemployment situation is the industrial need to 'tighten belts' and it becomes obvious that one is trying to sell a (possibly) unwanted product to very reluctant buyers!

Thus, whether you like it or not, you must become a salesman. You must identify your personal USPs (Unique Selling Points), research the market to find out what is wanted, improve the quality of your product to match the requirement, determine your publicity strategy, write your promotional material, evolve your sales technique, and *go out and sell yourself.* In short, realise that you are engaged on a *marketing campaign* in a highly sophisticated market and in the face of the severest competition.

The following table, based upon statistics maintained by the School of Management Studies of the Polytechnic of Central London and Management Selection Limited, will show you the size of the task you are about to undertake.

'*Middle Grade Executives*' (*Aged 45–52*)

	Trained in self-marketing	*Untrained*
Length of time to get a job	5–7 months	8–18 months
Number of letters written	200–250	300–500
Number of interviews	50	12
Number of jobs offered	5	1

Of course, these are only statistics. I hope you are the exception which will ruin them—it only takes one letter to get a job.

They are intended not to depress but to stimulate, to indicate the competition and to enthuse you to fight the odds and win. The interpretation that 'training' is the easy solution is fallacious. In the final analysis it is your personal qualities, ability and experience which are being judged and which will win you the job, but training is bound to be an aid to success. What I hope you have got out of the statistics is that:

1 It will take you longer than you think to get a job.
2 You are faced with heavy competition.
3 You must approach the problem scientifically by researching, determining strategy and individual tactics, and selling.
4 You have a great deal of hard work ahead of you, most of it tedious and repetitive.

Another problem you have to face is yourself. As soon as the boss has finished his 'Sorry, Charlie . . .' speech you find yourself in a state of *mental paralysis*, then you begin to *react* . . . the unfairness (why me?) . . . the ruthlessness (after 20 years) . . . the timing (on my birthday, at Christmas, Easter, just as I'm off on holiday) . . . leading almost to hatred of the boss, the firm and your colleagues . . . the shame of it. *Panic* is now setting in. How can I tell the wife? . . . What about the kids? . . . and what about MONEY? . . . the HP, (TV, deep freeze, car, house . . .). What will the neighbours and friends say? . . . they'll say I've got the sack. Now we have *self-pity*.

It takes a few days for the shock to pass until you are able to think about getting another job. You go to the office as usual, but in the train you no longer dwell longest on the sports pages, for you eagerly devour the advertisements. You don't like to discuss your problem with anyone; you couldn't possibly ask for help and advice. (You are probably reading this book with a false dust cover on it anyway!) You apply for the occasional job in the right salary bracket in the correct management structure and in an appropriate (to your house) location. You don't get a reply, or if you do it's a 'Dear Sir, we regret' letter. So you try again . . . and again. No luck, you say, and so you begin to *despair*. Months go by and your despair deepens, unti you begin to *deteriorate mentally* (although *you* don't notice it). You can't get a job, and now you can't even get an interview. Money is getting lower and the cost of living is getting higher. You can see no future at all. Now comes *fear*.

Nobody owes you a job, but you owe one to yourself and your family. Reason out a logical approach to the problem.

It is a sound military principle that before planning any action one must make an *appreciation of the situation.* This requires one to identify the enemy or enemies at each stage of the operation, to analyse their thinking, list the factors which will affect your plan, examine the 'courses open' and, finally, to work out a plan which gives the greatest chance of success.

Let us start our appreciation. Who are your 'enemies'?

Appreciating the situation

At the outset your aim must be to get an interview (you cannot sell yourself until you get eyeball to eyeball with the Personnel Manager). Hence, your 'enemy' is the reader of your letter. Clearly, it is necessary for you to know the enemy's thinking, to know management's approach to its problem of filling a vacancy and to know the roles which each of the key characters play in getting the right man for the job. You can then marshal the correct facts and formulate the correct presentation technique to put them over.

At the interview your 'enemy' changes to the other applicants. The majority of them have got to be knocked out in order that you attain your objective, i.e. to get on the short list. Therefore, you must know something of interviewee technique to help you to evolve your own successful sales method.

Your final 'enemy' is the boss, the directors or a panel of interviewers, for *they* are the decision makers. You need to know how they will think, what questions they are likely to ask and how they will evaluate you. Don't forget that you have not disposed of all the other candidate 'enemies', so you are having to fight a side action as well as a main battle. Your aim is now the job.

What are the factors which will affect your plan to get a job? Clearly, these must be personal factors which will be variable in every case, but listing them may help to crystallise the thoughts rushing about your mind.

Types of job

Have you the necessary knowledge and experience to get a similar or better job in the same field? Do you want to stay in the same field? Are you too old (or thought to be too old) for the 'rat race' of Big Business? Or would you prefer something on the 'Periphery' (Trade Associations, Bursarships, Education, Charities, Local Government, etc.). Have you the expertise necessary to put up your own plate in consultancy or the enthusiasm, courage and financial backing to run your own business?

Study all the advertisements in the national Press; they will give you hundreds of ideas.

Time available

How long have you got before salary and compensation income ceases? How long can you live on your capital? Analyse your budgets and do what your company has done. Cut back on the luxuries (except in one respect which we will discuss under the heading of Immediate Action in Chapter 8). Get cracking *now*.

Salary

What is your exact personal position in relation to living, education, housing, hobbies? Calculate the minimum salary you can accept, then evaluate your market worth (possibly deducting 20 per cent from your immediate assessment!). You now have a reasonable bracket in which to operate. Be prepared for something to go—the boat on the Hamble, the second car, but last of all your club membership! If you are around 50 then you must face up to the probability of a minimum 25 per cent drop in salary until you have established your contribution factor with your new firm.

Location

Do you own your own house? What about the mortgage? Can you sell it easily and satisfactorily with the Liberty curtains and the fitted carpets? How long will this take? What about your wife and your friends? Are you prepared to move? Look hard at the answers to these questions, because they could be such inhibitors that you may never get a job. You will have to determine the area of greatest opportunity for you personally and then consider your and your wife's reaction to moving home, to your living away during the week and to travelling. Does the job come first with you, especially at this stage?

Compatibility

When you get the offer of a job you will be placed in a very difficult position. Will you accept it or wait for the possibility of that better one in the pipe line? What are your objectives? Will you like the work, the people, the boss? Do you want to work for them? The essential ingredients of success are enthusiasm, skill and taking pleasure in what you are doing. This is not to say that you should turn down a job which does not fulfil all these criteria, but if you are in a difficult financial position, take the job and go on looking for the right one. After all, you are gaining experience every day, earning money and keeping yourself mentally alive—probably the most important factor of all.

Courses open

Your ultimate objective is to get a job. Your eye must be unwaveringly on this ball at all times, but we have already seen that you have intermediate aims to achieve this objective:

The aim of getting an interview.
The aim of getting on the short list.
The aim of winning the second (or subsequent) interview.
And then *The objective of getting the job.*

Now you can examine the courses open to you to achieve these aims. They are:

1 Reply to advertisements.
2 Send out round robins to selected companies for whom you would like to work and who might employ you.
3 Advise all your personal friends of your situation: after all, you may be doing them a favour by saving their recruitment costs.

It is the purpose of this book to guide you along a successful road to your ultimate objective by helping you to 'appreciate the situation' accurately, and to explore the methods to exploit the courses open.

CHECKLIST

1 The emergence of the 'two career' structure in industry.
2 Individual career planning is vital.
3 Personal development and training is *your* responsibility.
4 You must increase your contribution factor, over time.
5 Read and study to expand *beyond* your job.
6 The competition in the job market is fierce.
7 You must become a salesman. Identify your USPs, research the market, plan a marketing campaign and go out and sell.
8 It will take you 7 months, 250 letters and 40 interviews to get a job—if you are lucky.
9 Yourself as a problem: mental paralysis, reaction, self-pity, despair, mental deterioration and finally fear. These must be defeated.
10 Appreciate the situation. Identify your 'enemies', analyse their thinking, list the factors, examine the 'courses open' and make your plan.
11 Establish your objectives.

CHAPTER TWO

FILLING THE VACANCY: MANAGEMENT'S VIEW

Every company has its own systems and methods, especially in relation to personnel recruitment. As it is necessary for you to study the 'enemy's' thinking to formulate your own attacking tactics, I will describe the vacancy-filling process which is generally practised by most medium sized organisations. Variations in detail do not matter; my aim is to make a number of important points which are vital to your planning.

A vacancy in an organisation is created in one of two ways: either the present incumbent leaves (voluntarily or otherwise) or a new appointment is created. In either event (in the case of executive appointments), senior management is immediately concerned. Those members of the management team personally involved are the chief executive (i.e. the Managing Director, the Divisional Manager, the General Manager or whatever his title may be) the Personnel Manager, and the Organisation and Methods Officer.

It should be remembered that the chief executive is personally responsible for the profitability of his company or division and, thus, must accept the responsibility for the fitness of his organisation to do its task. He carries personal responsibility for the organisation and structure of the company. Any changes require his authorisation. The chief executive's principal staff officer in this respect is the O & M Officer. (Note that the O & M officer is in a staff relationship with other managers; he is *not* a line manager.)

The company's first line recruiter is the Personnel Manager. He too, is a staff officer, and he too can only recommend. One of his many duties is to draw up and submit for final selection a list of suitable candidates for the appointment. When a candidate has been selected, it is his task to tie up the legal and administrative ends of the appointment.

In the case of a new appointment being created the O & M Officer, together with the divisional manager concerned, recommends the new appointment to the chief executive. This will result in a detailed discussion of the need for the appointment, its role in the overall structure of the company and, of course, an analysis of the *job specification* which has been written by the O & M Officer. The Personnel Manager may well be included in this discussion.

Everyone realises that job specifications at executive appointment level are only guideline documents and have a very limited life, and therefore need periodic review. When one hires an executive, at a salary of say over £2500 p.a., one is hiring principally his ability to expand the job and to increase its profitability. Thus the new man's own ability, experience and interests will put different weightings upon the individual items of the specification from those originally intended by the writer. The justification for his weighting will be seen when one measures the result after a given period of time. That is why the job specifications of senior men should be reviewed frequently and progressively—another task for the O & M Officer.

Basically a job specification is a simple document. It states:

To whom the executive is responsible.
For what he is responsible.
The parameters of the job, which may include certain guidelines of *how* the job should be done.

As a side issue, it is a very illuminating exercise for a departmental manager to invite each of his section leaders (individually and unknown to each other) to write down what he does, and on separate pieces of paper what he thinks his colleagues do. In my experience, Mr A's personal job description covers several sheets, while those of his colleagues cover, at most, half a page. Furthermore, when one reads them all one sometimes wonders whether they are all writing about the same company, far less about the same people. Job specifications are very important because they effectively detail objectives and, to some extent, the systems being employed. A constructive analysis of them can lead to higher productivity and/or economies.

As soon as an executive leaves the firm his position comes under the microscope. The O & M Officer produces the answers to the following questions: is the appointment really necessary; can it be carved up and dispersed to other departments or executives; is this an opportunity to save on overheads; can the job be expanded to make a greater contribution; where should this job be in 5 years' time; do we want a higher or lower calibre of man to fill the vacancy; how does the appointment fit in with the company's development programme? The O & M Officer carries out a survey to answer these questions and makes his recommendation to the chief executive and the Divisional Manager concerned.

Then comes a meeting to determine whether the appointment should be filled, the type of man who should fill it and the approximate salary which he should be paid. These decisions having been made, the Personnel Officer goes away to write the *personal specification.* In most cases this is a very difficult task because the Personnel Manager knows that if he widens his personal specification too much he will get hundreds of replies to his advertisements, and if he makes it too narrow he may not get the right calibre of man, and thus will have to repeat the whole exercise. He has to pitch it just right. It is his wide knowledge of the executive market which will guide him, but basically he studies the job specification, and then lists the likely background and experience of the applicants he wishes to attract. As he writes he begins to build a physical and mental picture of the successful candidate who will eventually sit behind the vacant desk. Finally, after much rewriting he arrives at the personal specification. Remember, he has to bear in mind that he is not recruiting necessarily for the vacancy as it stands at present, but for the appointment as it will be in *x* years' time. Now he has the full picture—the *two specifications* which combined will form the basis of the advertisement he may have to publish. He then studies his existing staff.

At this point it must be assumed that no member of staff is suitable for this appointment so the decision is made to advertise. The Personnel Manager's next problem is to weld the two specifications into an advertisement. He then has to decide which medium to use—national Press, trade Press, institutional publications—to get the most accurate response to his requirement. The advertisement is then placed. The Personnel Manager knows that during the week after publication he will receive (for a job paying more than £2250 p.a.) between 200 and 300 replies. He also knows that of these applicants some 30 per cent will constitute a 'lunatic fringe', those who are obviously unsuitable for a variety of reasons but who are just 'having a go'. And why not? So they must be eliminated as quickly as possible. The remainder must then be categorised into '*probables*', perhaps of several grades related to experience, '*possibles*' and '*unlikelies*'. It is clear that the process will be time consuming and will extend over one or two weeks, and certainly will not require the Personnel Manager to devote his expensive time to this task. He is likely, therefore, to delegate the initial sorting task to one of his staff.

Most busy personnel departments possess the ideal lady to perform this function. She has been with the company for years, she knows the personnel systems, she knows how the Personnel Manager thinks and she is highly competent. Let us call her 'Nellie'. As you will see she is a Very Important Person, especially to the applicant. Let us see how she tackles the enormous task of sifting the replies.

The first thing she needs is a yardstick to measure the stature of the applicants. Remember her job is to categorise *not* to evaluate, and she is the first step in the elimination process. So she sets about creating her criteria (or it may be an established part of the selection procedure) by drawing up a *checklist* of the requirements of the job. She lists the points contained in the job specification, and then under a separate heading the necessary personal requirements. She then starts reading the mountain of letters. She is looking for detailed answers to the items on her checklist, and marking each letter accordingly—almost to the stage of 5, 7 or 9 out of 10. Piles of 'probables', 'possibles' and 'unlikelies' grow rapidly. Most organisations make a point of being courteous to applicants by acknowledging their letters, even if the acknowledgement is only a printed card saying 'Thank you very much for your interest. . . . If you don't hear from us within 10 days forget about it.'

The 'probables' are then passed to the Personnel Manager. His task is to select those likely starters for interview. He is, therefore, the eliminator-in-chief. At this stage he is looking for reasons why he should *not* see you, though at a later stage he will be looking for reasons why he *should* see you. He will evaluate you upon the facts you have given in answer to his advertisement, the way you have presented them, the logic of your argument that you are the most suitable candidate, the clarity and conciseness of your expression, and above all your personality, which must 'shine through'. If he does not find a sufficient number of starters among the 'probables' he will call for the 'possibles'; he may do this in any event to get a feel of the market and to check on Nellie.

By now he has some thirty probables about whom he wishes

to know more, so he instructs Nellie to send them all a form to complete and return. The purpose of this form is to obtain specific information in a standardised layout to make the evaluation of the individual more accurate, and checking of information easier. Are there discrepancies between the information contained in the letter and that listed on the form; previous employers' addresses and telephone numbers so that they can be contacted later if necessary; how much is he earning?

There are many types of application form, from the simple, single, basic information sheet to most complex forms of several pages in length which require a whole weekend to complete. Every company has its own ideas upon content, layout, format, etc., and consequently designs its own. Some even require one to write an essay on a given subject, others call for observations on how the applicant would deal with a certain problem. One must always be suspicious of those organisations which, after the initial interview, invite the candidate to express views in writing on a particular aspect of the job for which he is applying. Some years ago I applied for the job of European Marketing Manager of a company which was planning to expand into Europe. A day or so after the first interview I received a letter which ran something like this: . . . we are delighted to be able to tell you that you have been selected for the short list. . . . In order to help us make our final selection we would be grateful if you would detail your ideas of how you would expand our company into the European market . . . . I fell for it, and so did some twenty others I imagine. I never heard another word from the company, and I don't know if the post was ever filled . . . or even if there ever was a post. Certainly a cheap and effective way of obtaining many expert solutions to a difficult problem!

To illustrate the types of form which are in use I enclose examples on the following pages. The first is the simplest type, and probably the most common in various layouts, and the second, reproduced by kind permission of Management Selection Limited, an example of the more comprehensive personal history form.

Normally, a third of forms sent out are not returned (the applicant decides not to proceed further, or he has already got a job, or he has got the raise in salary he did not expect or a hundred other reasons) but those that are returned are married up with the original letter of application.

CONFIDENTIAL

THE A.B.C. GROUP LTD.

SENIOR STAFF APPLICATION FORM

Appointment applied for: ______________________________

PERSONAL DETAILS

Surname		Date of Birth	Age
First Name(s)		Married/Single	
Address and Tel. No.		Children	Ages
		Physical Disabilities	
Nationality		Today's date	
	When would you be available		

EDUCATION FROM AGE OF 12

Years		Name and address of School, College, and/or University	Examinations Passed	Subjects
From	To			

ADDITIONAL COURSES ATTENDED OR STUDIED

HOBBIES AND INTERESTS	
HOLIDAY COMMITMENTS	PTO

RECORD OF EMPLOYMENT

Please complete in chronological order, present employment first (excluding any service in the Armed Forces). Previous employers will not be contacted without your permission.

Month/Year		Company Address and Telephone Number	Appointment held	Duties	Salary p.a.		Reason for leaving
From	To				Starting	Leaving	

SERVICE RECORD

Years		Service	Arm of Service	Rank		Reason for discharge	Any further details (decorations, etc.)
From	To			On entry	On discharge		

First names in full .... *Please avoid BLUE ink* .... Surname (PLEASE USE BLOCK CAPITALS)

MSL *Personal History*

Reference /

None of the information which you give in this CONFIDENTIAL document will be disclosed without your permission.

Address

Date

Telephone numbers: private
(and times normally available)

business
(if we may ring you there)

Date of birth

Place of birth

Age

Marital status

Height

Weight

Have you any disability?

Ages of children, if any: sons

daughters

Which schools did you attend full-time from the age of 11?

.... from age .... to age ....

.... from age .... to age ....

.... from age .... to age ....

.... from age .... to age ....

Give the dates, subjects and results of any public examinations you took during this period.

Dates	
....	....
....	....
....	....
....	....

Give dates and details of any academic, professional or trade qualifications obtained.

	Date	*Qualification*	*Granted by*	*Subject and class (where relevant)*
i	....	....	....	....
ii	....	....	....	....
iii	....	....	....	....
iv	....	....	....	....
v	....	....	....	....
vi	....	....	....	....

How, when and where did you prepare for these (or other) qualifications?

i ....

ii ....

iii ....

iv ....

v ....

vi ....

In what languages, other than English, can you conduct business?

....

PLEASE TURN OVER

PRESENT APPOINTMENT
Or most recent, if none at present held* } *State which*

BASIC SALARY

Title

(i) on appointment

Date appointed

(ii) latest

Date terminated*

Other emoluments
(Bonus, profit share etc.)

Location of appointment

Employer

	Name	Total Employed
Group	....	....
Company	....	....
Division	....	....
Department	....	....

Pension terms

T/o (if known)

Public or private group/company? ....

£ ....

Fringe benefits
(Car, free house etc.)

Nature of business

OCCUPATIONAL EXPERIENCE. Start with the appointment immediately preceding that described above (whether in the same organi

Line no.	Year and Month from to	Employer's name: Location of job	Position held	Salary
1				
2				
3				
4				
5				
6				
7				
8				
9				
10				
11				
12				
13				
14				
15				
16				
17				
18				
19				
20				
21				
22				

Please describe your present or most recent appointment, indicating to whom you are responsible, and who is responsible to you. What do you consider to have been your major contribution in this appointment, and why? What are your main responsibilities and activities? Why do you wish to change? If you hold or have held any directorship, executive or non-executive, please mention it here or elsewhere.

ation or another) and work backwards. Include any employment in armed forces. Use as many lines for each appointment as necessary.

Nature of Business	Main responsibilities and activities	Reason for leaving	Line no.
			1
			2
			3
			4
			5
			6
			7
			8
			9
			10
			11
			12
			13
			14
			15
			16
			17
			18
			19
			20
			21
			22

Please write a short autobiography here which will help to explain the course which your career has taken. Please mention the things which have influenced you; the main interests you have developed; the achievements you particularly remember. If you have some ideas or ambitions for your future, please try to describe them.

How soon could you be free to take up a new appointment?..

....

Signature..
Will you please make sure that your name is printed at the top of the fr..nt page?

MANAGEMENT SELECTION LIMITED
Licensed annually by the City of Westminster

LONDON: 17 Stratton Street, W1X 6DB
01-493 3551

GLASGOW: 14 St. Vincent Place, C.1
041-221 7812

MANCHESTER: 474 Royal Exchange, 2
061-832 9424

BIRMINGHAM: Union Chambers, 63 Temple Row, 1
021-643 6234

DUBLIN: MSL (Ireland) Ltd
49 Upper Mount Street, Dublin 2
Dublin 65994

BELFAST: Property House,
11 Rosemary Street, BT1 1QA
0232-22350

MSL 110—2/71

The Personnel Manager now has all the facts, or rather he should have all the facts. He can select for interview. He is now both an *eliminator* and a *selector*. He is looking for reasons to throw out an application (and a badly written or presented application will give him just cause to throw it out), and at the same time he does not want to miss a good man—a man who is, perhaps, not entirely suited to the job advertised but may be very suitable for another appointment which he knows to be coming up in the future. He also has to consider how much time he (and his company) can afford to spend in interviewing, *and time means money*. This limits the number of people he will call for interview. Consider the following table for a moment:

The Cost of Interviewing
(Assuming *a 1 hour* requirement: reading-in, interviewing, reporting)

Interviewer's salary p.a.	*Rate per:* Hour	Day
£	£	£
10,000	6	42
7,000	4·20	29·40
5,000	3	21
3,000	1·80	12·60

So initially it will cost the company between £30 and £40 to interview ten candidates. Then follow the second and third interviews embracing the chief executive and the Divisional Manager at least. Add to this the cost of making the decision to fill the vacancy, the cost of advertising, the cost of Nellie's contribution and the cost of inducting the appointee into the organisation, and the total cost of filling the vacancy becomes enormous, as the following outline estimates show:

The cost of filling a vacancy

Decision making	£	£ (*say*)
Discussions on vacancy (chief executive, Divisional Manager, Personnel Manager, O & M Officer)	50	
O & M review survey (2 days)	40	
Writing specifications and advertisement	10	150
Reviewing existing staff; Discussions with managers; Interviewing staff	50	

The cost of filling a vacancy

Advertising		£ (*say*)
		500
Say *Daily Telegraph*, *The Times* and *Sunday Times* at least		(plus repeat advertisements if necessary)
Selecting	£	
Sorting letters: 3 clerk days	20	
* Acknowledgments	10	
Personnel Manager's selection for forms (1 day)	20	
* Sending forms and covering letters	15	100
Sorting forms and marrying up with letters	10	
Personnel Manager's selection for interview	10	
* Letters calling for interview (10)	15	
Interviewing		
1st (10) Personnel Manager: 2 days'	40	
Expenses (say 5 from provinces)	30	
Letters	15	
* *2nd* (5) Personnel Manager, chief executive, Divisional Manager, etc.:		350
1½ days	140	
Letters	15	
* *3rd* (3) As for 2nd: 1 day	100	
Letters and checking credentials	5	
Induction		
An appointee normally takes 3–6 months to get to know the company systems, policies, personalities and to begin to contribute, so at a salary of say £2500 p.a. this will cost the company about		1000
		£2100

* Includes postage.

So the minimum cost of filling a vacancy at this level will be about £2000

Clearly, with these figures in mind the Personnel Manager cannot afford to make very many mistakes, otherwise *his* contribution factor will be closely examined: so he has to be good at the job of accurate selection. He has the comfort of knowing, however, that it is not he who will make the final decision—that lies with someone else—but that he has to put up the correct men from whom to make the right selection. This is important, for now we see that the Personnel Manager is *not* the positive decision maker. He cannot say: 'Yes, you have got the job', he can only say: 'No, I cannot recommend you for the job'.

So he proceeds with his interviewing. His immediate task is to set you at ease (or as near it as possible), and then to get you talking about yourself, because it is then that your personality, knowledge and attitude will emerge. He has to get inside you to evaluate you. He develops his own technique of doing this, so the whole process requires depth study which we will examine later. There are a lot of lessons to be learned from this particular phase of 'enemy' activity.

And so the elimination process continues, until he arrives at his short list. He organises further interviews for you with the other key people . . . still eliminating . . . until the final decision is made. He then draws up the letter of appointment for the successful applicant, keeps the other short listees on the hook until he receives the acceptance, and arranges for your introduction, induction and training.

The diagram on the next page has been included to serve as a summary of this chapter, and as an *aide memoire* of the steps which are taken in filling the vacancy, and thus the hurdles you will have to jump to be successful. The next chapter will examine the procedure from the applicant's point of view and suggest actions which will help you to 'win the preliminaries'.

AUTOMOTIVE—KENYA/TANZANIA

One of East Africa's foremost public companies with substantial interests in the automotive industry has the following vacancies in KENYA and TANZANIA.

1. **Service Manager Tanzania:** Based in Dar-es-Salaam, dealing mainly with Land Rover but also with Volvo, Rover and Leyland Trucks. Attractive terms and conditions will be offered including total emoluments in the region of £T4,500 (Sterling equivalent £6,000/£6,500 approx). free car, Housing and Medical.

2. **Technical Instructor Heavy Commercial Kenya:** Based in Nairobi to organise and operate H.C.V. training programme. Total emoluments in the region of £K5,000/5,500 (Sterling equivalent £6,500 approx.). Company car, free medical and accommodation. Children's educational assistance.

3. **Workshop Manager Kenya:** Based in Nairobi to manage large Body Repair Shop. Total emoluments in the region of £K5,000/5,500 (Sterling equivalent £6,500 approx.). Company car, free medical and accommodation. Children's educational assistance.

General Conditions: Initial two year contract, overseas leave, local leave and passages. These terms allow saving as well as challenging opportunities in most pleasant countries with excellent climates.

Interviews in the U.K. early August, 1977. Applications giving full qualifications and experience to: **Managing/Service Director, c/o Court & Smith Ltd., 87 Woodbridge Road, Guildford, Surrey.**

15/7/77

we now need to recruit men and women for the following positions based at our Service Division conveniently located in Brentford.

ASSISTANT PROJECT ENGINEERS

Aged up to 50, you will be responsible for servicing of process plant—from diagnosis to advising on remedial action; preparing plans and tenders for the overhaul and conversion of existing plant, and ordering materials. You must be able to oversee work from conception through to completion.

Qualified to at least ONC level or with specific chemical engineering experience, your practical experience will possibly have been gained as a draughtsman or design engineer in a process industry.

TECHNICAL SUPPORT STAFF

These positions would suit responsible, methodical people with sound technical administration experience and the ability to read engineering drawings.

Probably aged 25 or over, you will supply a complete internal back-up service to the Project Engineers including collating information and maintaining relevant files. A good command of the English language is essential as liaison with outside suppliers and internal departments is involved.

Salaries are certainly competitive and supporting benefits are those associated with a major international company.

In the first instance please contact Dr. D. W. Carslaw, Permutit House, 632/652, London Road, Isleworth, Middlesex. Tel. 01-560 5199.

---

is for a minimum period of 12 months with bachelor accommodation provided.

Telephone Mrs Jones for an interview 051-227 2881.

Shaw Whitmore Fyffe Partnership,
Exchange Chambers,
2, Bixteth Street,
Liverpool.

SALES ENGINEER PUMPS

Established manufacturer requires a technical sales engineer for N.W. England. Ideally candidates will be in the 25/35 age group, having ONC mechanical (or equivalent) as minimum qualification. Product range comprises centrifugal and reciprocating pumps for sale to genral industrial, building services and consulting engineering outlets. Company car provided, pension scheme, &c. Please apply in writing to The Sales Director, Holden & Brooke Ltd., Sirius Wks, West Gorton, Manchester M12 5JL.

SENIOR ELECTRICAL DESIGN ENGINEER with at least 5 years experience in the U.K. on Building Services, required by Consulting Engineers—S.E. London. Telephone Maurice Baguley & Partners for appointment. Tel: 01-778 9311.

SENIOR SALES Engineer. Due to expansion the above vacancy has occurred with a leading and important international company in the field of heavy industrial fans and blowers, to assist sales manager and negotiate important contracts in the industrial field. A good knowledge of fans, blowers and industrial outlets is important. The position requires travel in U.K. and to the French works. An attractive salary and company car provided. Applications in writing to U.K. Executive, Solyvent-Ventec U.K., Petersfield Avenue, Slough, Berks.

WORK STUDY, industrial engineers. Senior personnel reqd for various long-term assignments throughout the U.K.—Chinal Management Services, tel. 021-353 8186.

Th
ot
re
sim
to
Re
Ja
Th
wil
de
sol
fro
bro
the
an
disp
gine
indu
is
App
qual
expe
to:
T
McC

CHECKLIST

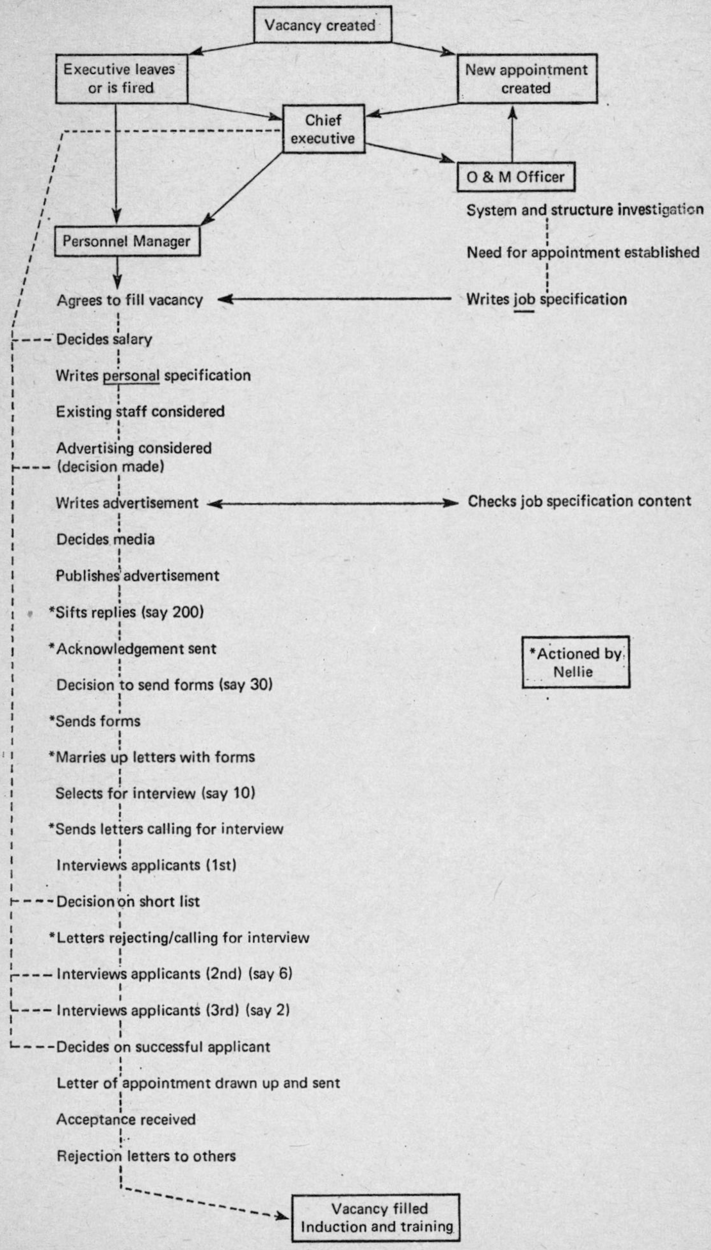
Vacancy created
Executive leaves or is fired
New appointment created
Chief executive
O & M Officer
System and structure investigation
Need for appointment established
Writes job specification
Personnel Manager
Agrees to fill vacancy
Decides salary
Writes personal specification
Existing staff considered
Advertising considered (decision made)
Writes advertisement
Checks job specification content
Decides media
Publishes advertisement
*Sifts replies (say 200)
*Acknowledgement sent
Decision to send forms (say 30)
*Sends forms
*Marries up letters with forms
Selects for interview (say 10)
*Sends letters calling for interview
Interviews applicants (1st)
Decision on short list
*Letters rejecting/calling for interview
Interviews applicants (2nd) (say 6)
Interviews applicants (3rd) (say 2)
Decides on successful applicant
Letter of appointment drawn up and sent
Acceptance received
Rejection letters to others
Vacancy filled Induction and training
*Actioned by Nellie

CHAPTER THREE

FILLING THE VACANCY: THE APPLICANT'S TACTICS

The previous chapters have traced in detail the thinking and actions of the senior members of the management team who are involved in filling the vacancy. From this we can list ten major points which will help you to determine your job hunting tactics:

1 The executives involved from the very beginning are:

The chief executive.
The Personnel Manager.
The Divisional Manager.
The O & M Officer.

2 There are *two* specifications for any job: the actual *job specification*, written by the Divisional Manager and the O & M Officer, and the *personal specification*, written by the Personnel Manager. Both specifications are combined to form the advertisement.
3 An advertisement may draw 200–300 replies at your level. Competition is therefore very heavy.
4 Nellie deals with the initial sorting process to produce 'probables', 'possibles' and 'unlikelies'. She works from a checklist drawn up from the two specifications.
5 The aim of your letter of application is to *get an interview*. 'This man I must see.'
6 The Personnel Manager is an eliminator. He cannot say 'Yes'; he can only say 'No'.
7 The aim of the first interview is to get on the *short list*. Later interviews are aimed at *the job*.
8 You are required to *sell* yourself at all stages.
9 Analyse the advertisement to determine what the advertiser *wants*. Identify the selling points you will make, in your letter and at interview.
10 Marshal the facts.

We have seen that the aim of the letter of application is to get an interview as the preliminary step to selling yourself in person. Your task is to get in front of the Personnel Manager. We have also seen that the key figures involved at the very beginning of the exercise are the chief executive , the Divisional Manager, the Personnel Manager and the O & M Manager. Immediately you see an advertisement which interests you, check your memory to see if you know any of these executives (or you can go to your local library and look up the company in *Kompass* or *Who Owns Whom*, etc.; more about this anon) and, if you do, write to them personally. The letter should be addressed to the executive by name, and marked 'for the personal attention of Mr . . .' or simply 'Personal and Confidential'. The letter then has a good chance of evading the 'Nellie system' and getting on the desk of the man who matters.

Round robins

Other factors which should feature in the achievement of your aim are the use of round robins and letters to personal friends who may be able to help you. Round robins constitute a mail shot to carefully selected organisations for which you would like to work, and which may have an opening for you. Clearly, it is useless just to write to the 'Top 500', and you must do your own research. Clarify your objectives (type of job, type of company, location, salary) and then draw up your mailing list —again from *Kompass*, local Chamber of Commerce list of firms in the area, *Who Owns Whom*, etc. Address your letter to the chief executive or the Personnel Director by name (spelled correctly, and with all his correct designation and qualifications, obtainable from most of the books mentioned above, or as a result of a telephone call to the company's receptionist). Your letter *must* be an original (i.e. not duplicated) and it must state concisely why the addressee should consider seeing you. To this letter you should attach your CV (curriculum vitae or the record of your career so far) the detailed compilation of which will be examined in the next chapter. As you are scattering your seed far and wide you must be prepared for the majority of it to fall on stony ground; only a small percentage will draw an answer—but then you might strike lucky. Companies *do* plan their operations well ahead, and Divisional Managers often ask their Personnel Manager to keep an eye open for the right man several weeks, or even months, before he will be required. Then your letter arrives on the Personnel Manager's desk. 'We haven't got anything for this chap at the moment', says the Personnel Manager, 'but I wonder if he would do for that job Bill is planning for our expansion into the Italian market . . . let's have a look at him'. You are in . . . you have got an interview . . . you are half-way to getting a job.

Note that it is a complete waste of time to send the Personnel Manager a CV with a covering letter which says: 'I would like to work for your company, I am very good. Please see my CV attached.' It is very difficult to visualise a greater insult to the Personnel Manager. That is like the salesman who knocks at your door and says, 'Here's my sales manual . . . I'll pop around to the local while you browse through it, and come back in an hour to take your order!' What would be your reaction? Clearly *you* must do the work. Your covering letter must show the Personnel Manager that you are good, and that you have certain things you can offer the company. By all means attach you CV but draw from it those sales points you wish to make.

It has been estimated that only 25 per cent of the appointments available on the market ever get advertised. Everyone in the recruitment field tries to keep recruitment costs down. We all have our contacts who may know of someone who could do such and such a job. A day seldom passes without someone asking me if I know of anyone who could do. . . . It is up to you to get in on such a network.

Personal friends

Another variation of this theme is the use of personal friends (who are not about to fall to the axe!). Do write to them telling them of your problem—again an original letter with your CV (indeed several copies for their friends) asking for their help and advice. He would be a very poor friend if he did not do something to help . . . an introduction, say, to a colleague or another business acquaintance. You are creating a sales force of your own, which is selling you! People are often diffident about 'using' personal friends in this way, but just think for a moment, you may well be doing *them* a favour and what is more saving them money. You will be pretty certain of getting a reply, and in my experience 75 per cent of such letters result in an interview.

Now turn to the advertisement. We have seen that there are two specifications, the job specification and the personal specification. Clearly, they are closely interrelated. The one states clearly what the applicant will be required to do, and the second what the writer *thinks* his background should be. In many cases the second is a compulsory adjunct to the first, but there are many others where the second specification does not necessarily follow—it is only a guide. It is your task to:

Identify the two specifications.
Decide which is the more important to job success.
Evaluate each of the items listed; place in priority order for the job.
Judge your experience against each item.
Decide whether it is worth applying (the Nellie system).
Write your letter answering the advertisement and *not* giving a rambling autobiography.

Advertisement analysis

These points add up to analysing the advertisement, and to do this accurately and quickly requires a great deal of practice. I commend that you study the advertisements in the Press and that you analyse three or four a day to begin with and then, once you have acquired the technique, concentrate upon those advertisements that interest you.

As a case study to indicate how the mind should work let us analyse a fictitious advertisement. This example is somewhat more verbose than most, but it serves adequately to bring out a number of important points. Please study the advertisement on the next page for a few moments.

Before you read on, jot down your own analytical thinking, the questions you would like clarified and the main points of your letter of application.

Are you quite clear what a Staff Manager does? It is quite incredible the number of people who apply for a job not knowing exactly what it entails. People confuse Staff with Personnel Management, Representative with Sales Agent, Production Controller with Works Engineer or Works Manager, Account

Executive with Brand Manager. Do make certain that you know what job you are applying for.

What do you know about the advertiser? Is it a reputable organisation, a good company to work for? Check its quotation

ADVERTISEMENT

STAFF MANAGER

Light Engineering Company

Applications are invited for the post of Staff Manager to the Croydon Accessories Company Ltd., part of the A.B.C. Group of companies. The Company is located at Croydon, and has some 2,000 employees of all grades engaged on the production of motor-car components and accessories. The Staff Manager will be responsible to the Company's General Manager for recruitment, training, welfare, negotiations with trades unions, and the formulation of company salary structure. He will receive advice and assistance as necessary from the Group Personnel Department. The successful candidate is likely to be aged between 35 and 50 and have had experience of staff relations; will be capable of organizing and directing the operations of a small department; will possess mature judgment and the ability to think constructively; and will be able to express his views clearly and concisely.

A starting salary commensurate with experience is offered, and the company operates a non-contributory pension scheme. There are prospects of promotion within the Group.

Letters of application, containing brief details of experience and qualifications should be addressed to:

The Group Personnel Director,
The A.B.C. Group of Companies Ltd,
A.B.C. House,
London, W1P 3FG

on the Stock Exchange (today's paper) if it is a public company; ask your friends. Only brief research is necessary at this stage, but it is essential to know what the company makes or does, and what capital it has and what the price/earnings ratio of its shares is (i.e. public public opinion of the company).

How does the location suit you? Are you willing to move house? Study a good map of Croydon and the surrounding countryside within 10 or 20 miles. Remember, you must search for your job in the area of greatest opportunity, so try not to be inhibited by location. A business associate was telling me the other day about a retired Admiral friend of his who had comfortably settled himself and his family in Henley-on-Thames. The Admiral wrote to my friend asking him to help him get a job. 'It must be near my home in Henley-on-Thames,' he wrote, 'and it must have to do with aircraft carriers!' My friend wrote back 'I'm sorry but I don't know of any aircraft carrier firms near Henley-on-Thames, but if you happen to see an aircraft carrier go past please let me know, and I'll institute enquiries right away.' No, that isn't a tall story, it actually happened. Even the most intelligent people fail to think through the location problem thoroughly.

What about the size of the Croydon company; does it appeal to you? It is obviously a medium sized operation, and the Staff Manager will very likely be a senior member of the management team. Certainly not a small fish in an enormous pond. The relative sizes of fishes to ponds may be important to you. Are you happy about working in a light engineering company? (at least it is not as noisy as a heavy engineering company!) and the products look attractive—radios and car accessories at special staff rates, and then, of course, the discount obtainable from the company's clients.

Now we come to the specifications. Let us disentangle them so that we can analyse our chances of success.

Job specification

Responsible to the company's General Manager for: recruitment, training, welfare, negotiations with trade unions, and the formulation of company salary structure.

Those are the five points Nellie will be looking for under this heading. Against each write down your own experience which proves that you can handle each aspect. In addition, list any other experience or attributes which would show your capability of expanding the job—remember, you may well be applying for the job as it will be in *x* year's time.

Personal specification

The successful candidate is likely to be: 'aged between 35 and 50, experienced in staff relations, capable of organising and directing . . . a small department, possess mature judgment, think constructively and express his views clearly and concisely.'

Do a similar exercise. List the points and justify your claim that you match the Personnel Director's image of the man behind that particular desk. Visualise what the advertiser wants, and then try to match that image.

If you have scored more than say 7 out of 10 then you have a good chance of getting an interview, so start sharpening your pencil to draft your letter of application.

There are, however, one or two points in the advertisement which, as an applicant I would like to query—not to be included in the letter, but to be brought up during the interviews. Now is the time to list them while you are analysing the advertisement.

Queries on the advertisement

The advertisement states that the Staff Manager will be responsible to the company's General Manager, that is to say, *not* to the Group's Personnel Director. Why? Is there a personality problem here between the General Manager and the Group Personnel Director? Perhaps not, but the situation needs clarification. Does the Staff Manager have two bosses? If so where lies the dividing line of 'line' and 'staff' relationships?

Is this a new appointment or has the previous incumbent made a nonsense of a delicate situation? (Obviously, this will influence your tactics at interview.) What systems are already in operation? Does the Staff Manager have a hand in the formulation of Company Personnel policy, or is he really only an outstation clerk? What type of staff (male, female, grades) are employed, and to which unions do they belong?

Why such a wide age bracket? What was the Personnel Manager's reasoning when he wrote 'between 35 and 50'? Clearly, age does not matter very much provided that his criteria (of maturity and experience) are met. What is important to him is that the successful applicant must not be too young to be acceptable to the staff and to his managerial colleagues, and he must not be too old to be accepted into the company's pension scheme, and yet he must be able to offer many years of valuable service to expand and grow with the job. In short, the age factor does not matter too much in this case. Obviously, there are many situations where it matters a great deal, so it is up to you to determine the weighting being placed upon it by the company, through your own experience and intelligence. If you are 55 and you see an advertisement for a 'dynamic overseas sales manager who will be expected to spend 6 months of the year "in the air", with a proven sales record etc., etc., aged up to 33', you would be pushing your luck if you expected to get an interview. My message, therefore, is as regard age brackets as flexible (within reason), and do not rule yourself out because you are a year or two over the top. Have a go: after all, it only costs you three pence postage. Do not bother, however, to apply this thinking to appointments in Government service. If a Civil Service advertisement states 35¾ years old on 17 September it means just that; so don't waste your time and money.

How much is the job worth? Why has the company refrained from defining the salary? There could be a number of reasons for this:

> They may be 'trawling' the market because they don't know the 'going rate', or they want to see what the advertisement will produce.
>
> The company does not want other members of staff (or even perhaps competitors) to know how much a particular member of staff is being paid. After all, an employee's salary is strictly a personal matter between him and the management.

But, of course, the question of salary will appear high on your list of queries, and the fact that the salary has not been stated gives the applicant plenty of room to evaluate and negotiate at interview.

The company operates a non-contributory pension scheme. What are the details of the scheme? Normally, a non-contributory pension scheme is worth 5½ or 6½ per cent additional to your salary, but a study of the details of the scheme is important for you. (The number of years of service, expressed as a fraction of 60 or 80, dependent upon the type of scheme, multiplied by the average of the last 3 year's salary, is the normal formula.)

Prospects of promotion? It is always nice to know that such prospects exist, but of course no company can guaranteee that they can be fulfilled. However, as the advertiser has made a point of inserting that statement in the advertisement it is a reasonable matter to pursue later. You will need to know in which field such prospects are envisaged, whether at home or abroad, and whether a location move is likely.

The advertisement requests you to send *brief* details of experience (some even vaguer organisations ask applicants for the salary required) and qualifications to a specified address. Do as the advertiser asks. The details must answer the advertisement, be brief and be sent to the correct address. It is strange how many people will write to Croydon Accessories Ltd and not to ABC Group Ltd. Quite apart from the fact that your letter will probably be thrown away, such an action can be quite embarrassing. A friend of mine replied to an advertisement through a box number, with a carefully worded application giving details of his present job without mentioning his company, and proving that the job he was presently doing exactly matched the job specification in the ad. The reply he received was from his own personnel department. It was *his* own job being advertised! This is only a preliminary reconnaisance on both sides. The Personnel Manager wants to judge whether you are a 'starter'; he will get all the information he wants on the form, and at the interview, and you do not want to put all your goods in the shop window. You must have other things to sell when the time comes, but you have got to titillate the interviewer's imagination and make him say: 'This man I must see'.

CHECKLIST

1 When you see an advertisement which interests you check whether you know any of the 'top brass'. If you do, write to them personally.
2 Use round robins and letters to personal friends with original letter plus copies of your CV. *You* must do the work.
3 Identify the two specifications in the advertisement, evaluate, judge and visualise. Do you fit the Personnel Manager's vision?
4 Analyse the advertisement in detail: the job, the company, the location, the size of the 'fish', do you fit the job and personal specifications? List the points that justify your claim. Judge whether it is worth applying for. Don't worry too much about the age factor.
5 Identify and list any queries you have, in readiness for the interview. Prepare your questions in priority order.
6 Do as the advertiser asks in the advertisement.

CHAPTER FOUR

MARSHALLING AND PRESENTING THE FACTS

I have stated that the job hunting process is a carefully planned marketing campaign. In this chapter we will examine the preparation and presentation of our promotional literature:

The personal career record.
The Curriculum Vitae.

Your career record

The first step is to marshal the facts, and from them determine your strengths and weaknesses, identify your USPs and then present them to the best advantage. Let us start at the beginning. Compile a personal record of your career. Get a *large* sheet of paper for the following columns:

EDUCATION

Dates	*Ages*	*Schools/College/ University, etc.*	*Examinations passed and results*	*Additional information*

List all information chronologically, as for example:

1930–1940	7–17	Blankaster School	Oxford School Cert. 7 subjects (3 credits)	School Prefect Captain of Athletics
1947–1950	24–27	University of London	B.A. (2nd class) History	
1953–1955	30–32	XYZ Correspondence College	Diploma in Marketing	

and any further education and Courses attended.

CAREER

Dates	*Ages*	*Employer*	*Appointment and to whom responsible*	*Number of people responsible to you and starting and ending salary*
1941–1947	18–24	The Army (Regt.)	From Private to Major (Commissioned1942)Paratrooper. Italy & NW. Europe Regt'l Officer responsible to the Commanding Officer.	Normal duties of a platoon (36 soldiers) and company commander during war time (M.C., Mentioned in Despatches)
1947–1950	24–26	Bloggson Ltd. (address and/ telephone no.)	Trainee Executive Responsible to the Office Manager	After training, i/c Orders and Enquiries Dept. (2 executors 3 secretaries, 4 clerk/ typists) £500–6700.

and further detailed information to present day.

Great care must be exercised in the compilation of your career record. All the facts *must* be correct. If you have been working for sizeable organisations, the Civil Service or the Services you will be able to obtain a photocopy of your personal history sheet which will be held on file; if not then you will have to rely on your memory. This record will prove invaluable because it will become the permanent factual record of your life, and you will be able to refer to it at any time. Incidentally, I believe that everyone should keep such a record up to date throughout their working life so that all facts are recorded and thus cannot be overlooked. Be very careful with the responsibilities and duties column. As you will see, this will contain the most important information, as it details your experience. Put down everything you can think of: special responsibilities, projects handled, major visits to other companies, overseas trips, negotiations, sales (both direct and indirect), committees, notes on confidential reports—everything.

The final section of the document should be headed:

ADDITIONAL RELEVANT INFORMATION

FOREIGN COUNTRIES Dates and places lived. Knowledge of the peoples socially, commercially and culturally. Knowledge of the country, its laws, geography, etc.

LANGUAGES SPOKEN Degree of fluency, conversationally, commercially, technically. Competence in reading, writing and speaking.

PERSONAL ACHIEVEMENTS Treatises, books or articles written and published. Lectures read, TV and radio appearances. Outstanding sporting achievements, and anything else at which you excelled.

HOBBIES AND INTERESTS List everything, highlighting your main interests.

ANYTHING ELSE

You will appreciate that to compile such a comprehensive record of your life will take some time. Take it slowly. Go over it time and again. Miss nothing. Everything you have done in your life is important, has been a factor in building your character and experiences, and you may need to refer to this information at any time. You will certainly need it to move on to the next stage.

Now that you are equipped with all the facts you must analyse them to see what you personally add up to. Your objective is to identify yourself, your strengths and weaknesses. You will probably evolve your own method of introspection, but obviously the process will begin with a detailed study of what you have written. Then, as one method of achieving your objective, I suggest that you add two further columns to the career section of your record sheet:

Personal Evaluation	
Job successes	*Job failures*

Go through each important job you have held and judge whether your personal contribution to the end result was a success or a failure, and why. This is your own personal assessment, which need not necessarily confirm the view taken by your boss at the time. Identify each project you handled, and note down the end product; the pay-off; the profit! then identify which of your qualities was displayed to make it a success or a failure. Do this exercise with care and you will see that five things emerge:

Your practical strengths.
Your characteristics.
Your knowledge gaps.
Your most successful 'job area'.
Your strongest contribution factor.

You have thus identified your personal USPs, so now see how to present them.

The curriculum vitae

This document, call it what you will—CV, personal history, details of . . ., etc,—is, without doubt, the most important document you will ever write. To you it is worth an income of *x* thousands of pounds a year, and tens of thousands of pounds over the next *y* years. To a potential employer it is a case study in depth which will be paramount in his judgment of you. Your interview and your future employment will hang upon this document. It is a key, a door opener; and it is your 'sales manual'.

As you know, every salesman (and *you* are now a salesman)

must have a sales manual—a document which shows the product(s) he is selling, its characteristics, its specification, its advantages over competitive products and the reasons why it will satisfy the prospective purchaser's requirements. This is what your CV *must* do. It must, therefore, contain details of your background and personal information, your record of employment, your experience and what you have done with it, your unique selling points, your contribution factor and an insight into your character. All this to be expressed logically and in a language which management can understand. You will be judged to the *n*th degree on this document because it will be regarded as *the* best example of the work of which you are capable. It must be laid out logically, its text must be clear and concise, and it must contain the story of your life *on one sheet of paper*. Every word must be weighed, and every full stop and comma in the correct place. The document must become alive, you must shine through to make the reader say: 'This man I must see!'

The appearance of this document is of the greatest importance. Correct headings and sub-headings, adequate margins, clear straightforward type face, beautifully laid out and immaculately reproduced. Yes! reproduced. The aim of the CV is to open as many doors as possible; it is your publicity brochure, and it will be disseminated as widely as possible. Its task is to create as much interest in you as a person as possible. When a prospect has read your CV he should know all there is to know about you—he even has a good idea what you look like. So, if a CV is tailored to any specific advertisement, it immediately becomes suspect. Has the applicant bent all or any of the facts to match this job specification? If so, he himself is suspect! This is the basic fact-containing document. Those facts required for any specific job are extracted from the CV and written up accordingly, in the letter of application.

Statistically speaking you will need 250 of them. I strongly recommend that you have them typed and reproduced professionally, preferably by being printed offset litho. Any good typing agency will do this for you at a cost of about £3 to £3.50 for 250 copies. Surely a worthwhile investment.

As to layout there are so many schools of thought that it is important for you to evolve your own format. The method you adopt does not really matter as long as you keep to the principles stated above. However, to give you a base line from which to work I suggest the following headings (with notes on them) for your consideration.

Headings for a Curriculum Vitae

FULL NAME IN CAPITALS

Date of birth. Age. Marital state. Children (showing dependants).
Home address and telephone number.
Business address and telephone number if appropriate.

EDUCATION AND QUALIFICATIONS

School, years, examinations passed.
Further education, years, qualifications.
Courses attended or undergone. Results.

ARMED FORCES SERVICE

A *brief* statement showing dates served, in which service, etc., highest rank attained (at age . . .), type of engagement, where served.

CIVILIAN CAREER

A *brief* history in narrative form showing the development of your career, the companies you have worked for and the major appointments held.

EXPERIENCE

This is the selling paragraph. Put in as much 'punch line' information as you can under appropriate headings, for example:

Training
Sales
Marketing
Management and Administration

GENERAL

In this section bring in as much as you can of the 'additional relevant information' part of your career record. Close with a clear statement of your *aim* for the next *x* years.

Examples of various types of CV are included at Appendix A.

You are bound to get conflicting advice about CV writing and format because everyone has his own view of how it should be prepared, and even how it should be used. This is a good thing. Many points of view are expressed which you can distil to your own particular requirement, and create your own *individual* selling document. What is important is that you must make your CV interesting and alive. Remember that the Personnel Manager is your 'enemy' at this stage. He is looking for ways to eliminate you. You must, therefore, capture his interest and hold it so that he reads everything you have written. It is the experience of hundreds of people who pass through my training courses every year that this is the most difficult document in the world to write—and get correct. It requires drafting, editing and re-editing many, many times before it is moderately acceptable. A presentable CV takes about a fortnight of intensive part time work. Let us, therefore, look more closely at its content and try to arrive at some do's and dont's.

Every document must have a *title*, and the title must reflect the subject matter. *You* are the subject of the CV so your *full* name must appear at its head. If you happen to have any awards or decorations do not include them at this stage. Presumably they were awarded as a result of something you have done; they are therefore an 'end product' and should be shown against the appropriate item of your experience. You will be hired against your record of achievement and an evaluation of your potential. Awards and decorations are therefore important—but in their proper place.

The essential of a CV is to say the most in the least number of words. For example, at the beginning of the document do not write 'Date of birth', just write 'Born 13.3.23 (48 years)' or Married, 3 children (1 at school)'; or 'Bachelor'. This gives the picture clearly and quickly. Do not go into irrelevancies such as numbers of marriages, ages and sex of children. These facts will emerge by a skilful interviewer if it is necessary for the company to have this information; all that is required at this stage is to give the overall picture. The statement that one child is still at school could have some bearing on your responsibilities, financial commitments or your mobility, and thus it is important. Your address is clearly vital, but one line only. There is no need to put in 'Tel. No.'; a telephone code, or place name, followed by a number is obviously a telephone number.

The education qualifications paragraph is important because it indicates your background and shows the start point of your adult life. The remainder of the document shows what you have done with it. State the type of school, public, grammar, etc., and, if it is well known, its name in parentheses. Anything in brackets in such a document as this means 'this is not terribly important; you don't *have* to remember it'. Continue with the years you were at school also in parentheses, and follow on to further education. Make a point of highlighting the examinations you passed and any qualifications you obtained, and the age, in brackets, at which you achieved them. Make quite clear your background and achievements. If you have come up the hard way then the greater is your achievement, and this will be recognised. Courses you have undergone are important as they show that you have continued your education throughout your life, and that you have kept your brain receptive and retentive, quite apart from the knowledge they have imparted. Try also to show that you have kept abreast with your job, and that you have shown interest in, and enthusiasm for, your work.

Now come *the career paragraphs*. It is useless presenting a chronological list of firms and jobs. Dates are relatively unimportant. For example '1961–1962' is meaningless since it could mean 1 month or 24 months. What is important is the actual length of time you did the job, e.g. 6 months or 3½ years. The main point about the career paragraph is that it should paint the outline of your career to give the reader an introduction to the vitally important paragraph headed experience.

The *experience paragraph* contains the sales material: your proven USPs, your knowledge and experience, the number of people responsible to you personally in each section, and above all the contribution you have made to your employers, i.e. the end product. This information must be given as concisely as possible. When you have written this paragraph wait a while, re-read it and see how many questions it answers positively and with no ambiguity. Every sentence should produce one or more answers to questions. Think of the questions the reader must ask, and ensure that you have answered them. Avoid adjectives: 'wide' or 'considerable experience in...' are common howlers. By whose standards? You are pre-empting the reader's judgment. 'I have written several articles on this subject' is another. How many; what happened to them; were they any good; is this pure bluff? are immediate questions in the reader's mind. Keep editing. It is very difficult to edit one's own work successfully. The more one does so the more confused one becomes . . . is it better to get someone else to do it: your wife (probably the severest critic of all, especially as to fact), a friend, your boss (perhaps he will be so impressed he will give you a raise immediately) or best of all a chief executive or Personnel Manager friend (apart from the great value of his opinion it could be a good way of getting an interview or even a job!).

Identify carefully the sub-paragraph headings from your experience. These items are what you are offering for sale as individual items, or as a whole package. Make sure that your phraseology is that of a middle or senior executive, and that you use terms which management will understand. By this I mean that you must avoid specialist jargon, technolese, militarese or civil service gobbledegook. Yet you are advised to use those words and phrases which the reader will be looking for under a given heading. For example under the heading of 'training' the reader would be looking for the following 'OK words': 'planning courses, tailoring to requirement, lecturing, course administration, arranging specialist lecturers, the following grades of student . . . , (and the pay-off) so many students qualified'. Give a lot of thought to what the reader will *want* to read, and then draw from your experience to satisfy as much as you can of it. You are literally writing your own job specification and then answering it.

And so we reach the *final paragraph*. The object of this paragraph is to show the reader the type of man you are. Where, outside your job, your interests lie. What extraneous achievements you have accomplished (played Brutus in *Julius Caesar* or climbed the north face of the Eiger), where you have travelled, the languages you have picked up (formally or otherwise). This is the pushover paragraph to make the reader say: 'This man I must see'. And believe me, everyone has something hidden away in his memory which could be the subject of a book . . . so unearth it! Finally (or if you prefer it at the very beginning of the CV) state your *aim*. Perhaps it is to 'seek more challenging responsibilities' or 'to start a new career'.

Now a few don'ts:

Don't waffle.
Don't bend the facts.
Don't mention salary required.
Don't include the salaries you have earned (you will be required to do this on the form).
Don't write an autobiography.
Don't submit a chronological list of jobs.

Don't write anything which may be detrimental to you and your objective.

Study the examples of CVs given in Appendix A.

CHECKLIST

1 Prepare your career record:

Education.
Career.
Additional relevant information.

2 Make a personal evaluation of yourself and your achievements. List your strengths and weaknesses, and arrive at your USPs.
3 Prepare your Curriculum Vitae, your sales manual:

Heading Personal details Armed forces career Civilian career Experience . . . . General	This is the best example of the finest work of which you are capable.

4 Be sparing with words.
5 Show your background and your achievements.
6 *You* must shine through.
7 No chronological list of jobs.
8 No autobiography.
9 Write selling material (watch style). Make sure you have an 'end product' to every paragraph.
10 Make the CV live, and the reader say: 'This man I must see'.
11 You will need 250 offset litho copies.

CHAPTER FIVE

LETTERS OF APPLICATION AND THE APPLICATION FORM

The aim of the letter of application is to get an interview. This fact should be in the forefront of your mind at all times. You are *not* trying to get a job—you are trying to get an *interview*. If you bear this thought in mind while you are writing, it will make all the difference to the way in which you write the letter, what you put in it and how you express yourself. Cast your mind back to Chapter 2 and recall the Nellie system of categorisation and the Personnel Manager's role of eliminator-in-chief. Your task is to overcome those hazards. You have seen the need to analyse the company's requirement and to identify the image of the successful candidate in the Personnel Manager's mind. It is your job to meet the requirement and to match that image.

Your letter is your first contact with your potential employer, so it must create the correct impression. Let us dispose of some basic points before we start drafting our letter.

Stationery

Play safe by using a plain white, good quality paper, quarto or A4 in size with matching envelopes. A printed address is acceptable provided the typeface is not too ornate. Do not use a letter head with your name printed across the top as this is considered ostentatious in the extreme.

Hand written or typed

Both Nellie and the Personnel Manager are used to reading typescript, and the latter is a very busy man. No matter how good the handwriting it requires much more concentration to read than typescript and is, therefore, a source of irritation. Remember that your letter may have to be read in a train, on an aircraft, in the bath . . . anywhere when the Personnel Manager has a spare moment . . . and most inks run when tea or water is spilled on them! You will also need a copy of your letter to refresh your memory before the interview . . . so on balance *type* your letter unless the advertiser specifically requests you to reply to his advertisement in your own hand. Finally, a typewritten letter gives a good business-like impression.

Phraseology

Refer to the facts you have marshalled in the experience paragraph of your CV and write up the sub-title paragraphs in great detail, drawing heavily on your career record. Edit and rewrite until you have concise, polished sentences, expressing what you have to say in easy-to-read language. You will then have built a master reference 'library' which you will use over and over again. This will be of great help when you are writing your many letters, because, let's face it, you will have to say the same things hundreds of times in the course of your campaign. Some of the boredom will thus be removed from this tedious task, and your output of letters will be greatly increased.

You are now ready to *draft* your letter. I am sure that it would be impertinent of me to tell *you* how to write a letter; not only that, but you can probably do it much better than I can. Furthermore, it is important that you write your own letter because *you* must 'shine through'. The Personnel Manager is judging you, personally. There are, however, a number of important points concerning the format and content of a good letter of application.

The address

Do not use a business address or the address of your club. The former prompts the question: 'Hasn't he got a home?', and the latter the comment: 'What a snob!' Just use your private address. Don't forget to date the letter.

The addressee

It does not matter whether you put the addressee's name and address at the top or the bottom of the letter, but it is important that it appears somewhere—important for you to refer to later.

Dear Sir

If the advertisement instructs you to write to a specific person by name, or if you happen to know the Personnel Manager personally, then do so (e.g. Dear Mr Jones), but never, never adopt the Civil Service or Services greeting of 'Dear Jones'. This is guaranteed to irritate, and the letter will probably go straight into the waste-paper basket. (After all, even a criminal is referred to in the Press as Mr Jones until he is found guilty, when quite suddenly he becomes 'Jones'.)

Subject heading: Staff Manager, Croydon Accessories Ltd.

Put the subject heading of your letter boldly in the centre of the page and underline it. This helps the Personnel Department staff when sorting the mail, and makes it quite clear for which vacancy the candidate is applying. (The company may be advertising for two Staff Managers, one at Croydon and the other for their factory at Bootle.)

Opening sentence

Again be helpful. Most large companies analyse the effect of their advertising in various media, so they need to know in which publication and on what date you saw the advertisement. I suggest that your opening sentence is something like this:

> 'I have read with interest your advertisement in today's *Daily Telegraph* for a Staff Manager at your Croydon factory, and request to be considered as a candidate.'

The body of the letter

This is the selling paragraph in which you must answer the advertisement (remember Nellie's checklist), and give the Personnel Manager enough information to whet his appetite for more. Include nothing to your detriment, and only those facts of your career which are relevant to the job you are applying for. Do *not* write an autobiography. Be careful how you express yourself. A typical statement is 'I regret that I am 52 years old and that I am therefore outside the age bracket mentioned in the advertisement'. The writer has eliminated himself before he starts. If you are outside the age limit just don't draw attention to the fact—your age will come out later, certainly when you have to fill in the form—because your task is to get over the Nellie hurdle first. Another common phrase is 'I am retiring from . . .' Never use the word 'retiring' as it creates a picture of a doddery old boy leaning on a farm gate watching the sun go down. Use the word 'leaving' and do not explain the circumstances which will come out at the interview. 'Redundant' is another word with an adverse connotation. The use of it places the writer at a great disadvantage as it prompts the question 'Why him?' The message is: choose your words and phrases carefully to give a good impression, and to convince the reader that you can do the job efficiently and make no reference whatsoever to salary, fringe benefits, etc. Those will be discussed at the interview.

Be careful not to oversell. If, for example, you are going after a job at £2500 a year, and you write yourself up as a £5000 a year man (which you may well have been) then you will frighten off the Personnel Manager. Tailor what you have to offer to the size of the job, but give enough bait to make the reader interested in *you* and your potential.

Do not put all your goods in the shop window (e.g. do *not* enclose your CV) but retain plenty in reserve. Remember your aim. Always be positive, and *always, repeat always, write the truth.*

Closing the letter

After your selling paragraph it is a good idea to make it clear to the reader that you are available for interview at *his* convenvenience.

You have completed your first draft. It now requires editing and polishing. Read it carefully and then answer the following question: 'If I were the advertiser would I want to see this man?' Continue re-writing until the answer is 'Yes'. Be on the look out for spelling mistakes and grammatical errors. When you are satisfied with your final draft, type it out making a carbon copy. Be sure that you type your name below the place for your signature, read it through once more, and then sign it. It is amazing how many applicants forget to sign their letters. Type the (correct) address on the envelope—if to a box number check the figures carefully—insert the letter and please don't forget to stamp it; or to post it!

The marketing approach

So now your campaign has started. You are writing highly professional letters in reply to advertisements, but do not forget the other methods of publicising yourself:

The round robin.
Your personal friends.

The importance of these approaches has already been impressed upon you, so considerable thought should be given to drafting such letters. Like the letter in answer to an advertisement, these letters must be originals and addressed to individuals by name.

The essentials of the round robin letter are that it must:

Show that you know what the company does.
Show that you are interested in working for it.
Show where your experience could be of value.

The steps to success in this situation start with basic research in the local library to find out what the companies you select manufacture, the name of the person to whom you intend to send the letter (spelled correctly) and the address of the company. Remember, you are selling a *very expensive* product, so care in everything is important. You will undoubtedly be judged by the layout, phraseology, format and content of your letter. So you must get it right first time; you will not get another chance.

You should aim to write at least three letters every day, and you will probably have some ten letters 'in the air' at any one time.

In these two circumstances it is perfectly acceptable to attach your CV (drawing from it the main selling points you wish to put over to each particular addressee and making it the 'body' of your letter). In fact it is a good idea to enclose half a dozen CVs with the letter to your personal friends, and two copies with the round robin letter, just in case the addressee wants to pass them on!

Regard the whole operation as a marketing campaign and, as a marketing manager would do, allocate a certain capital *investment* in promoting yourself. A possible self-marketing budget would be something like this:

Self-Marketing Budget	£ (*say*)
CVs printing cost	5
Stationery, letterheads, envelopes, carbon paper, files, etc.	10
Postage	10
Typewriter	25
	—
Total investment	50 (at least)

This sum should be seen as an investment which will be well recouped if it means that you get a job more quickly. Work it out as a percentage of your first year's salary when you get the job you are after. Self-advertising in the Press or specialist publication produces nil returns in the current employment climate. It should only be considered if you are a rarity whose expertise is greatly sought after—and then a letter to appropriate prospects may suffice.

Personal organisation and method

Your campaign must be supported by an adequate administration. You will find it is essential to keep a carbon copy of every letter you write, and to keep all correspondence neatly filed by type of job and by company. A geographical breakdown may also be necessary if you are going after jobs all over the country or even overseas. You will have to work out the best system for your own case, but there are a few major points which you should observe:

1 When answering an advertisement, cut out the advertisement from the paper, and glue it to the carbon copy of your letter of application. In this way you will not lose the original advertisement, and it will always be at hand for easy reference.
2 Purchase an alphabetically indexed concertina file in which to file your letters (all correspondence with each company stapled together).
3 Buy a stiff covered (thick cardboard) file cover in which to keep your bulk supply of CVs in *immaculate* condition. An ordinary manila folder will do for those dozen CVs you will carry in your brief-case at all times.

4 Draw up a JOB HUNTING RECORD. This I think important for three reasons:

MARKET ANALYSIS Showing the types of job you are going after, the salary structures, the locations and the dates when certain things happened. This should indicate the profitable and unprofitable areas of your campaign, and thus will help you reformulate your tactics as necessary.

BRING-FORWARD SYSTEM Your campaign record will also serve as a brought-forward system which you will find essential for keeping tabs on your actions, and for 'prodding' prospective employers and contacts.

MORALE BOOSTER The fact that you will have to discipline yourself to maintain your record will keep your mind active, add interest to your task, keep you up to date, and above all allow you to review the position easily and quickly. You will, therefore, find a sense of daily achievement which will encourage you to continue the battle with optimism and enthusiasm.

It is up to you to devise the most appropriate layout for your job hunting record, but to start you off on the right track I suggest that you draw up two forms which in essence would cover:

Sheet 1

ADVERTISEMENTS JOB FINDING AGENCIES

Salary Scales
£
1750–2250
Half a page of jumbo-sized paper each
2251–3000
Etc.

Sheet 2

ROUND ROBINS PERSONAL FRIENDS

A straightforward chronological list

Suggested layout of these forms are on pages 49 and 50

SHEET 1

JOB HUNTING RECORD

Salary Scale 1750–2250

ADVERTISEMENTS							JOB FINDING AGENCIES							
Company/Appointment	Salary offered	Dates				Job offer	Agency	Company/Appointment	Salary offered	Dates				Job offer
		Letter	Form	Interviews	B/F					Letter	Form	Interviews	B/F	
Bloggson Ltd (Office Manager)	2000	2/1	5/1	10/1, 17/1	~~20/1~~ 22/1		PeE Reg	(Association Secretary)	1750	20/1				
A B C Ltd (Staff Manager)	2250	15/12	20/12	2/1, 9/1, 15/1		✓	A–K	Smith Ltd (Office Manager)	2100	10/12	15/12		1/1	
							Officers Association	Johnstons (Sales Rep.)	2250 + car	15/1	25/1		7/2	
Salary Scale 2251–3000														
Jacksons Ltd (Sales Manager)	2750 (+ car)	2/2	10/2	15/2, 20/2	~~20/2~~	✓	MSL.	?	2500	Tel 5/1	10/1	15/1	20/1	
Salary Scale 3001+														

SHEET 2

JOB HUNTING RECORD

ROUND ROBINS						PERSONAL FRIENDS					
Company/ Appointment	Salary	Dates			Job offered	Name	Dates			Introduced to company	Job offered (salary)
		Letter	Form	Interviews			Letter	Form	Interview		

The job hunting record will, of course, refer to your filing system, which will contain all the information you want. A further sophistication will be to extract the 'hot' prospects on to a separate form, on which you would be able to go into greater detail as an *aide memoire*.

Filling in the application form

As we have already seen, there are many types of application form, almost as many as there are companies. Some companies follow the recruitment procedure explained earlier (i.e. advertisement, letter, form) while others invite the applicant to write for an application form at the outset. There are no rules for completing the application form but there are some obvious things to do. These are:

1. Always write the truth, especially concerning your age, salaries you have earned and the length of time you have been with a company. All these, together with the actual posts you have held and any military ranks you have reached, are easily checkable. NB.
2. When you are filling in the form, imagine that this is the first contact you have ever had with the company, whether you have been in touch previously or not. The reader requires you to complete the form because he wants the information in a uniform way to make comparison easier. So give him everything.
3. Make a point of highlighting your experience which is particularly relevant to the job advertised, hence detailed reference to your advertisement analysis—what does the employer want?—what does he do?—how does he do it?—how do you see the job being done?—how can you improve on his ideas?—what is his image of the successful candidate? Ask yourself these questions and then answer them. Write what the reader *needs* to know.

I think it is a good idea to attach your 'sales manual', i.e. your CV to this form, even though a large part of the information will have been duplicated, mainly because if you have done your 'homework' properly, the CV will be a very powerful sales document, and the reader will be able to form a very accurate picture of you, and as you have written the CV you will shine through.

Your objective is to get an *interview*; 'This man I must see!'

Take time to fill in the form. Draft your answers to the questions, taking the information from your personal career record, but be careful to express yourself in the best way possible—always with the requirements of the job in mind. Type your answers on the form, keeping a carbon copy (you can usually remember the questions posed, especially when you have gained some experience); better still, take a photocopy of the whole form, and file it in your concertina file. You will certainly need to refer to it if you are called for interview.

And so you plod on . . . writing letters, filling in forms, improving your written sales technique with every letter you write. It seems an interminable time before something happens but then, strange as it may seem, you will suddenly get a number of letters like this:

THE ABC GROUP LTD

Tel: 01–580–0471 A.B.C. House,
London, W1P3FG

Pers/SM/1422 15th September, 197–

Dear Mr Armitage,

Appointment of Staff Manager
Croydon Factory

Thank you for returning the completed application form so promptly. We have studied the form (together with your original letter of application) with interest and would be very pleased if you would attend these offices for an interview on Thursday, 20th September at 3.30 p.m.

Please confirm this appointment with my secretary by telephone, and on your arrival ask the receptionist for the writer personally.

Yours sincerely,

John Jones

Group Personnel Director

A 'strike' at last! Now on to the next phase of the campaign —the interview.

If the date/time is not convenient then telephone and fix one which is mutually convenient.

CHECKLIST

1 The *aim* of the letter is to get an *interview*.
2 Plain white A4 paper, typewritten, carbon copy required.
3 Prepare your phraseology until you have concise, polished sentences, which you will use over and over again.
4 Draft and edit before you do the final copy.
5 Use your home address, never 'Dear Jones, subject heading.
6 Answer the advertisement. Analyse the advertisement and meet the requirements. Don't oversell, and don't write an autobiography, don't mention salary, fringe benefits, etc. *WRITE THE TRUTH*. No CV. Sign, stamp, post.
7 Ask yourself: 'If I were the reader would I want to see the writer?' Continue drafting until you get the answer 'Yes'.
8 Round robins and letters to personal friends require a number of CVs to be attached.
9 Support your campaign by good administration:

    Carbon copy (with advertisement affixed).
    Adequate filing system.
    Job hunting record.

10 Take time to complete the application form, imagine it is your first contact with the company, highlight your experience relevant to the job. Attach your CV.

A further thought for more senior posts

It may be a good ploy to submit your application a few days after the advertisement appears; your letter is more likely to be near the top of the pile when Nellie gives it to the Personnel Director.

CHAPTER SIX

THE FIRST INTERVIEW

The aim of the first interview is to *get on the short list*. So, you have been invited to attend an interview. When you have got over the shock go straight to your filing system and extract all the previous correspondence you have had with the company, take a new manila folder and label it with the name of the company. Insert the correspondence, and stick a blank sheet of white paper on the inside of the left hand cover. Head this sheet of paper '*research information*'. You are now ready to proceed.

Re-read the letter carefully, boldly underlining the following salient points:

LOCATION OF INTERVIEW It may not be at the address to which you have already written.

DATE AND TIME OF THE INTERVIEW It is amazing how many candidates turn up for interview at the correct time, but on the wrong day!

NAME AND APPOINTMENT OF THE INTERVIEWER The 'enemy' has appeared. You will need to find out as much as you can about him and his organisation as quickly as possible.

INSTRUCTIONS What has Mr Jones told you to do? and then do it! (In this case it is to confirm the appointment by telephone, *not* in writing.)

These points may sound elementary, but I commend them to you because so many silly mistakes are made by applicants for jobs, especially when they are under strain, or as we hope in your case, are dealing with a number of invitations to interview at the same time. You cannot afford to make mistakes. Everything you do from now on must create the most favourable impression. Do not eliminate yourself before you even get a chance to sell. Get the interviewer on your side.

You now move into action. This stage is called *research*. You will appreciate that an interview is a two-way affair. The interviewer is trying to find out all about *you* to decide whether you are a suitable starter for the job. But you are trying to find out all you can about the *company and the job* to decide if you want to work for it. The more research you can do before the interview the better—it will give you the basic information which will aid your eventual decision, and at the same time create a very favourable impression of you in the mind of the interviewer. I suggest that you tackle the research stage under three headings:

Research about the company.
Research about location and communications.
Research about your selling points.

Let us examine each of these in detail.

Research about the company

This should start immediately—indeed at the very moment you telephone to confirm the appointment. When you speak to the interviewer's secretary ask her to send you all the company's public relations literature and its latest annual report. This will be favourable to you as it will detail the company's activities, its products, its markets and outlets, and a lot of additional background information. Most companies will be only too pleased to do this. Without a doubt you will get top marks for initiative in the interviewer's book when his secretary tells him about your request. Another important point is to confirm with her the correct pronunciation of the interviewer's name—and make a phonetic note on the research sheet in your company file (e.g. Lascelles rhymes with tassels; or Scrope pronounced Scroop). If you have been asked to confirm the appointment in writing, then get this information by telephoning the company's PR department.

Next, you get down to desk research. You need factual, down-to-earth information. Your Bank Manager (or Stockbroker) will have, or can get for you especially if he thinks that you are about to invest some money, Moodies or Extel cards on the company. These cards give a wide range of information about the company (financial state, type of business, products, etc.) and can be obtained for a very small fee. Alternatively, go to your local library and look up the company in Moodies *Investment Handbook* (a quarterly publication), or the *Stock*

Exchange Yearbook, which will give you everything you need: capital employed, number of employees, subsidiaries, locations, monthly share prices, company developments and other details of immense interest. Then there is '*Who Owns Whom*', and *Kompass*, which is particularly useful for listing companies —including unquoted companies—in a given geographical area. At a later stage a visit to Companies' House (55–71 City Road, London EC1) to study the company's annual reports, Memorandum and Articles of Association, and accounts may well be rewarding. If you live outside London write to Companies House for this information.

From these sources you can build up a very good background picture of the company, its size, turnover, profitability, organisation, products, major outlets and even how much it pays its directors. You can then determine its growth rate (or otherwise) over recent years and make an intelligent forecast as to its future prospects, which may, of course, have a considerable bearing upon your own future with the company. Very important is the fact that all this information will give you the basis of sound and intelligent questions which you can ask at the interview. You will also be able to enter into any discussions with confidence, and an intelligent appreciation of the company's problems, especially those in connection with the job you are after. You can now begin to analyse in depth the demands the job will place upon you, and you can anticipate the 'technical' questions you are likely to be asked by the interviewer. List such questions on the Research Sheet for future reference.

Finally, ask your personal friends what they know about the company. Is it a good company to work for? Does it pay well? Are its products well thought of? Is it a reliable supplier? Who are its major competitors? And what is the general impression of the company? You must end up with a 'feel' of the organisation.

Research about location and communications

It is important that you know three things:

1 Exactly where the interview will take place?
2 Where you will be working for the next x years?
3 How long it will take you to get to (1), and what are the problems in travelling to and from (2)?

If you are not absolutely sure where ABC House is, then telephone the company and ask. The receptionist will tell you the easiest way to get there, and give you clear directions for your journey. If you have a full address then you can look up the exact location in any good street directory which you will find in your local library.

It may not be essential at this stage but certainly at some future date you will have to make a personal reconnaissance of your actual place of work. You will have to examine the best route to get there, and if you are going to travel by train or car I strongly recommend that you make a trial trip *in the rush hour*. Your experience will help you to decide whether or not to move house, or indeed if you really want the job.

Research about your selling points

With all the information you now have, coupled with the deductions you have made about the company in general and the job you are after in particular, you must now examine your own selling points to identify those which are the most important for you to promote *in this case*. Remember, when you are at the interview you are a salesman. Your aim is to get on the short list, and so your method must be to outshine the other candidates. Any salesman will tell you that the most important part of selling is the preparation of his presentation. This is what you must now do. Prepare a list of a few major points, say four or five, which you want to put over to the interviewer. Points which will impress him with your ability to do the job (not only now, but as it is likely to be in *x* years time), points which will show to advantage your enthusiasm, knowledge and personality. Keep the list of these points in your file because, before the interview you will have to memorise it, to ensure the interviewer gets everything that is necessary for him to know in order to make a favourable report upon you.

There will always be opportunities during the interview for you to make your points—perhaps during one of those inevitable silences, or in answer to a question or when you are asked if there is anything else you would like to say or ask.

The first interview

So the great day arrives. The previous evening you have

checked through your company file to see that you have everything you will need: The advertisement, copies of: your letter of application, the form, and any other correspondence. The research sheet, your list of selling points (including any specimens of your work which may be needed), the list of questions you wish to ask the interviewer, and of course, spare copies of your CV. Your suit has been pressed, your shoes polished, and your tie carefully selected (this is often a good 'ice breaker' as it can be a ready-made talking point). You set off with plenty of time in hand to allow for the vagaries of transport systems, climatic conditions or other hazards which invariably beset applicants. Your aim is to arrive at the appointed place about five minutes early, well briefed on the job you are applying for and on the company itself, (read up again during the journey), composed and on 'top form'. Report to the receptionist who will probably pass you on to the interviewer's secretary.

If you have a few minutes to spare before being summoned to 'the presence' then use them to advantage. Chat to the secretary —about generalities of course—but it is amazing how much you can deduce about the boss (and the company) from the secretary's attitude, quality and presentation. She, too, is a VIP. Her boss may well ask her the impression she has formed of certain candidates. If the secretary is of the uncommunicative type, then glance through the company literature which is certain to be lying around. The object is to keep your mind active and away from the interview ahead of you so that you remain calm. You must avoid nervousness, or at least showing it.

The moment comes. The secretary opens the great man's door and ushers you in (don't forget to thank her, by the way, it creates a good impression) and introduces you to the 'boss'. The next thirty seconds are the most important of the whole interview. First impressions *do* count—the remaining forty-five minutes are spent in checking them out. A polite interviewer will come towards you, welcome you and invite you to sit down. A good interviewer should not interview you across a desk (to avoid any inferiority/superiority undertones) but will try to get you at ease as quickly as possible by using a pair of arm chairs and a coffee table.

Every interviewer has developed his own technique, but the objectives are the same:

REDUCE THE CANDIDATE'S NERVOUSNESS TO THE MINIMUM Every interviewee must be nervous—this is accepted, but the more nervous he is the more inhibited his brain is. It is the interviewer's task to 'get inside' the candidate to find out how good he really is. It is only when he has banished the candidate's nervousness that he can do this.

GET THE APPLICANT TO TALK The best interviewers are the best listeners. While one is listening one can assess in depth.

ELIMINATE The personnel manager can only put forward a limited number of short-listed candidates, so he is looking for reasons to eliminate all the time. (An over-talkative salesman so often talks himself out of a sale!)

In order to achieve these objectives interviewers normally open the batting so that the candidate can get accustomed to the surroundings, probably by offering him a cigarette (do take one if you smoke, but cigars and pipes are usually taboo), and a cup of coffee or tea. Pleasantries like 'easy to find us', 'a good journey' and the 'weather' over, the interviewer usually tells the applicant 'something about the company'. He is feeding in information to see later how much has stuck, and to watch for the intelligent questions his facts are designed to promote. It is in this area that your research will begin to pay off. Note that he must be conscious of security of information. He must not say too much; after all you may be a 'plant' by a competitor, or even a free-lance journalist or, unlikely as it may seem, even an industrial espionage agent. He will certainly elaborate the job specification, and spell out the requirements of the successful candidate. By this time he will have gained your interest, and be studying your enthusiasm for the job, and he will assume that your nervousness level is now at its lowest. Slowly, he will turn the tables on you, by getting you to start talking. He will, therefore, invite your questions on anything he has said. No, wait for it! Confine yourself to questioning him upon the company, its organisation, and the job. Don't start feeding in your USPs yet—the time will come.

This is where you have to develop your own technique of handling interviewers. Great skill is needed to put over the impression you want the interviewer to have of you. Just consider for a moment. How long is it since *you* have been interviewed successfully for a job? How many years have you been sitting on 'the wrong side of the desk'? We have seen that this job hunting business is a campaign, a competition no less. If you were a sportsman entering for a competition what would you do? Surely you would practise against likely opponents, and you would train. You must do the same in this serious business. You need a great deal of practice to deal with the wide variety of interviewers you are going to meet if you hope to be successful. So the message is: develop your own interviewee technique by going out and getting as many interviews as you possibly can, regardless of salary, location or even job. Just *go after* the interviews, gain the experience, develop your sales and interviewee technique so that when the jobs you really want come along you are in top form and thus will have a chance of winning.

To return to our interview. The interviewer wants you to talk, so if you help him to achieve this desire he will surely begin to warm to you. But again, you must gain the experience of knowing just how much to say, and how to say it to this particular type of man. Don't oversell, and don't talk yourself off the short list. Eventually the interviewer will return to the attack. He will draw on the homework he has done on you, and start questioning you upon the statements you have made in your letter of application, your CV and the application form. He is now in the elimination stage. He is trying to find causes for striking your name off the list. The questions he will be asking himself will be concerned with verification of the truth, the depth to which your knowledge and experience goes, and your ability to fit in with other members of the firm—and thus the assessment of your contribution factor. It is during this phase that you start feeding in the prepared points you want to get over. Never let an opening slip past. Fill the odd silence (some are deliberately created just to see what you will do), turn a question to bring in an USP, counter a question with a question to make a 'one-upmanship' point. Everything you say must be *true* and *positive* and to your personal advantage.

Every interviewer has a crop of favourite questions which he will use in differing forms at every interview. Here are some common ones which are bound to occur from time to time. They are 'hardy annuals', so have the answers well prepared:

Why are you interested in the job advertised?
This is a wonderful question for you to answer. The interviewer is playing right into your hands. What a magnificent chance for you to get over some of your USPs. Answer showing that your experience and knowledge are ideal to make a success of the job.

I see that you live at . . . How would you get to the office?
You have got to be positive about this. If the travelling will be difficult (thus you may not contribute as much as someone who does not have this problem) what do you propose to do about it?

Why are you leaving your present job?
Be truthful. Your answer will eventually be checked with your previous employer. No matter what the circumstances of your leaving your present company, *never* 'knock' an employer. Your loyalty, integrity, sincerity and truthfulness are at stake here. Don't set out to damn yourself though!

What plans have you for your future career?
Have this one worked out. Outline your ultimate and stage objectives, and then show how you can achieve them within the company and how your contribution will be to the benefit of both parties.

What level of salary are you looking for?
Be very careful with this one. You can so easily price yourself out of the job (too high a figure—and even too low a figure—may eliminate you). If you have done your advertisement analysis thoroughly, you will know what the job is worth on the open market, and therefore will be able to quote a realistic bracket, adjusted to your own contribution, of course.

If you were appointed to this position, how would you set about . . . (then follows a hypothetical problem)?
Be cautious. Take time to think out an answer. The interviewer does not really expect a correct answer because he appreciates that you will not know the issues involved within his organisation. He is watching how you react to a 'fast one'. Of course, if you are acquainted with such problems then use the question to your advantage. Your research into the company will help a

great deal, and you will be able to score 'one-upmanship' points again.

There are many more questions which interviewers dream up: note them for future reference, and between interviews prepare a well thought out answer. Another reason for interviewee technique training, so keep at it.

While all this is going on it is your task to assess whether you want to work for the company. An interview is a two-way affair. You will have to answer, to yourself, the following questions if you are offered the job!

Do I like the firm, its products, the people?
Can I do the job? What are its parameters?
Can I improve my (and the job's) contribution to profitability?
Will I like the work? Is the responsibility sufficient?
Is there a career here?

Consequently you will have to prepare questions which will produce the answers to these questions. This meeting is exploratory on both sides, the Personnel Manager will expect to be questioned, so think them out carefully. There are, however, a few don'ts.

Please don't ask questions about fringe benefits, holidays, hours or work, bonuses, removal expenses, expense accounts or other jobs in the company. Companies have their own policy and system for the payment of expenses to reimburse candidates for out of pocket charges. The normal practice is that the interviewer will ask you if you wish to claim and will arrange payment through his secretary there and then. Obviously, this becomes an important matter if you have had to travel a long way, and if you have had to buy meals, so in such cases (if the interviewer has not mentioned the point) have a quick word with his secretary on the way out.

Do not hide the fact that you have other irons in the fire; the interviewer will expect you to have if you are job hunting seriously. Finally, don't interrupt, and don't interview the interviewer.

So it is over, and all you have to do is to wait. But keep on with your campaign. As soon as you get home think over the interview and how you could have improved on it. List all new questions.

CHECKLIST

1 The *aim* of the first interview is to get on the *short list*.
2 Open a company file: previous correspondence, advertisement, copy application form, research sheet, selling points, questions, spare CVs.
3 Re-read letter, underline salient points: location, date/time, name of interviewer, comply with instructions.
4 Research about the company: PR material, annual report, Moodies/Extel cards, reference books in library.
5 Anticipate the interviewer's questions, and those you will ask. Prepare lists.
6 Research about location and communication: location of interview, location of job, travelling time and conditions. Reconnaissance.
7 Research about your selling points. You must sell and score more points than your competitors. Prepare list of points you wish to put over (ability, enthusiasm, knowledge, personality).
8 Smart turn out. Make sure you know where to go. Ensure that you have everything you want in your brief-case. Allow plenty of time to arrive five minutes early. Arrive composed.
9 Read yourself in during the journey. The job, the company.
10 Avoid nervousness as much as you can. Warm to the interviewer and he will warm to you.
11 The first thirty seconds are the most important. First impressions *do* matter. Do smile, and do use the interviewer's name.
12 Help the interviewer to do his job, but remember he is looking for reasons to eliminate you. Tell him how you can solve his problems.
13 Develop your own interviewee technique. Learn how you want to handle interviewers, and how to get your selling points across.
14 Know the answers to the favourite questions, and expand the list by your own experience.
15 The interview is a two-way affair. Find out what you want to know about the job, the company, and the prospects. Your job is to *obtain* as well as to *give* information.
16 Think before answering a question. Sell yourself well. Be careful of the 'oversell'.

17 Be frank and truthful, and remember the 'don'ts'.
18 Remember that the Personnel Manager cannot say 'Yes', he can only say 'No'.
19 Think over the interview and make notes on how you could have improved upon it. Apply these thoughts next time.
NB 20 Be professional.

CHAPTER SEVEN

SUBSEQUENT INTERVIEWS AND THE LETTER OF APPOINTMENT

The *aim* of subsequent interviews is to *shorten the list* and to *get the job*. Your campaign is doing well. You have been on several first interviews, and you have decided that, so far, the ABC Group job is the one you would like best. You are on tenterhooks waiting to hear from them. This morning you received the following letter:

CROYDON ACCESSORIES LIMITED
A member of ABC Group of Companies

Tel: 01–686–4812

Pers/SM/IDM

Technic Street
Croydon
CR9 1NR
Surrey
25th September, 197–

Dear Mr Armitage,

Appointment of Staff Manager

Further to your recent interview concerning the post of Staff Manager of this company, I shall be pleased if you can attend a further interview at these offices at your earliest convenience. Will you please telephone my secretary for an appointment at a mutually convenient time within the next week.

Yours sincerely,

I D Marshall

General Manager

You have done extremely well for you are now in the last half dozen or so. You know that the second interview has been arranged, probably, to make the final selection, or possibly to compile a short short list. In either event, you will be on the home straight and will, at last, meet the man who can say: 'Yes, that's the man I want!' You are now about to sell to the decision maker—the man who matters. Clearly, you are now after the *job*, and these two factors will make a great deal of difference to the way you approach the problem ahead of you.

Read the letter again, carefully. Notice that the letter is from a different address. It is not from head office but from the company where you will work. It was written by the General Manager, the man for whom you will be working if you get the job. The letter instructs you to telephone the boss's secretary to fix an appointment which will take place at Croydon. Work out two or three convenient times, and then 'phone her and fix the date and time. Now you must complete your research if you have not already done so. Be quite clear on everything detailed in the last chapter, and prepare a new list of points you want to raise. This may be your last chance of gaining the information necessary to the decision you may have to make: 'Should I accept the job?'

You may have to get your duties and responsibilities clarified. You will certainly have to get the salary position and starting date cleared up. Now is the time to be looking for those fringe benefits, identifying the hours of work, allowances, holidays, car, pension scheme, and all the other things which will make the job more attractive. But be careful; this interview may have been called only to shorten the list. There may be another planned for the finalists. You will have to feel your way very carefully; you don't want to put the boss-man off. I suggest that you list the points you want cleared up, and leave it to the interviewers to bring them up during the interview. If they don't do so, and you feel that the climate is right, then you have every right to ask for such information. But be tactful. The interviewers are still trying to assess you in relation to the job and your personal contribution. They are comparing you with the other candidates

It is most likely that you will be interviewed by a panel, of which the General Manager and the Personnel Director will be members. Other senior members of the company will probably be present. You are now faced with a 'group presentation' and must be prepared for questions to be fired from all quarters. Your 'enemy' in this situation is clearly the other candidates. Your tactics, therefore, must be designed to show that:

1 You are the most suitable candidate for the job because your potential contribution will be greater than theirs.
2 You outshine them in respect of enthusiasm and personality.

You are now after the job!

At this point your interviewee technique, born of practice, will come into its own. You will have learned how to present facts to people, to register the impact of your words upon the listeners and to swing your attack to get the best effect. You will have learned how to listen, to sort out the wheat from the chaff and how to present your experience and achievements to the best advantage. But make no mistake you will not be 'conning' anyone because the interviewers will be very switched-on,' 'ten-out-of-ten' men. It is your *ability* which will, in the final analysis, win the day. But good presentation of facts is 50 per cent of the battle and, after all, that is at least 50 per cent of the requirement of a good senior executive.

Subsequent interviews take much the same pattern as the first, the same preparation will be needed on your part and the same 'drill' will be adopted. However, because there are more people involved, it could have a more formal air about it. On the other hand, you will already have met the Personnel Director and you know that you rate pretty highly with him. To some extent, therefore, he is on your side. At least he is a friendly face, and will introduce you to the others.

The questions you will be asked will surely cover similar ground to those posed by the Personnel Director (the boss-man will want to hear your answers himself—and, of course, check your answers with the first interviewer's brief and personal assessment form in front of him). But he will go into much greater depth in regard to your ability, contribution potential and personality. Remember that he will be interviewing these candidates who are the cream of the applicants. The questions will probably probe deeply into your past experience to identify the extent of your achievements, and move to the field of 'How would you deal with such and such a problem?'

Your task, before the interview, is to anticipate such questions and work out the detailed answers. This you should be able to do from your previous contact with the company, your analysis of their needs and their thinking. Obviously, your interviews with other companies (the 'training interviews') will help you a great deal. One cannot, however, anticipate them all, so be prepared for the 'googly'. Don't panic; just take your time. Don't try to 'flannel' your way out of a tricky one. If you really don't know the answer say so, but try to turn the point to something you do know about—and make another USP.

When all candidates have been interviewed, the panel will confer. The members will discuss each finalist in detail, and everyone's opinion will be expressed. The candidates will be placed in order of merit, and the decision taken to whom the first offer should be made. The letter of appointment will then be drawn up and mailed.

Let us assume that you are the chosen applicant. You will then receive the following letter:

CROYDON ACCESSORIES LIMITED
A member of the ABC Group of Companies

Tel: 01-686-4812
Pers/SM/IDM

Technic Street
Croydon
CR9 1NR
28th September, 197-

Dear Mr Armitage,

Appointment of Staff Manager

Further to your recent interview concerning the above appointment, I have much pleasure in offering you the post as from 15th Nextember 197-, at a starting salary of £2,500 per annum, (Two Thousand Five Hundred Pounds) which will be subject to annual review. Salary will be payable monthly (less deduction of income tax and National Insurance contributions) direct into your bank account.

You will be entitled to four weeks' paid holiday a year (apart from national holidays); dates being subject to negotiation on the basis of an executive roster. In the event of absence due to sickness, salary will continue to be paid for three calendar months or such longer period as may be decided by the Board of Directors.

The factory works on a two-shift basis; normal office hours are from 0830 to 1700, Monday to Friday inclusive, with an hour's break for lunch. The Staff Manager is expected to be present within normal working hours, and outside these hours as his duties require.

The provisions of our non-contributory pension scheme are detailed in the enclosed booklet. You will be required to undergo a medical examination for admission to the scheme; arrangements for this will be made by the Company.

The appointment will be subject to termination by three months' notice in writing on either side.

I would be glad if you would confirm your acceptance (or otherwise) of this appointment by return of post, and I sincerely hope that you will be able to join us on Monday 15th Nextember 197–.

Yours sincerely,

I D Marshall

General Manager

This is a normal letter of appointment which conforms to the requirements of The Contracts of Employment Act of 1963. This Act requires that the conditions of employment be set out in writing to every employee and lays down minimum periods of notice for termination of employment. The points that a letter of appointment should cover are:

1 A firm offer of the appointment (stating who the employer is, if there is any doubt).
2 Starting date.
3 Salary to be paid, intervals of pay and how paid.
4 Holiday entitlement.
5 Sick pay entitlement.
6 Office (i.e. working) hours.
7 Details of the company pension scheme. (Usually given in an enclosed booklet.)
8 Period of notice of termination of employment.
9 Request for confirmation (or otherwise) of the appointment.
10 Signature of the official offering the appointment.

With reference to the period of notice to be given by the employer, the Act lays down the following minima:

Over 5 years' service	4 weeks
2–5 years' service	2 weeks
Under 2 years' service, (but over 26 weeks)	1 week

However, in the case of managerial posts a minimum of 1 month's notice is usually given, and more likely 3 months. Lengthier periods are the subject of negotiation between both parties.

When you get your letter of appointment, study it carefully to ensure that all the conditions of service are covered and, in addition, that any points you have agreed at the interviews (e.g. salary review after 6 months or promotion to the Board after a certain period) are included. So many people become disenchanted with their new employers after a short period because promises (real or imagined) have not been fulfilled. The employer should put all such agreements in writing, and it is your responsibility to see that they are correctly stated. Remember, once you have accepted the appointment terms as set down in the letter of appointment you are legally obliged to adhere to them, as indeed is the employer. If you have any objections or queries, get them sorted out with the person offering you the job. Never rely on 'understandings'.

If you are conducting this campaign as recommended, quite suddenly you will have a number of these firm offers of jobs on your desk (this is your original aim, remember?). You will then be able to sit back and analyse each offer. Evaluate the pros and cons of each job: salary, prospects, compatibility, job satisfaction, location, travelling, etc., and then make your decision. And once made, *throw* yourself into it. If you have any spare time between acceptance and joining use it wisely, by continuing your research into the new organisation, gleaning as much information as you can about personalities and systems, and do a detailed study of its markets and competitors. The more information you can get at this stage the greater will be your contribution when you join. The company will certainly help you all it can. Collect as much reading matter as you can and then, if possible, get away for a few days' holiday to recharge your batteries. (Reading-in will stimulate you, *not* run you down.)

To revert to the offers sitting on your desk—before you have made your firm decision. It often happens that a timing problem arises at this stage. Suppose, for example, that you have received the letter of appointment from the ABC Group and that you have recently attended a final interview with another company. At this interview you were given to understand that you are on the shortest possible short list, and it is your calculated opinion that you will be offered the job. You feel that you would far sooner have the second job, but you have not yet received the vital letter. What to do? How can you delay the acceptance of the first (firm) offer while you wait for the possible offer from the second firm.

Think through the problem from management's viewpoint. The ABC management will know that you are conducting a campaign to get a job (it will regard you as a fool if you are not!) and must, therefore, have other offers or potential offers in the pipeline. After all, the ABC management think you are good so why shouldn't other companies? Clearly, ABC Group will be sympathetic to your problem. My advice, therefore, is to be thoroughly straightforward. Telephone the Personnel Director (or better still go and see him if he can spare the time) and explain the position, requesting time to think the problem over. (Don't tell him that you would sooner have the other job, though; be diplomatic.) If he is really keen to have you, he will certainly agree to a reasonable time lag, but don't forget the problem which has now arisen for him. If you eventually decline the offer, then he has to approach the Number 2 on his short list, and the Number 2 may slip through his fingers if the time lag is too long. The Personnel Director will then have to start the whole tedious recruitment process all over again. The reasonable delaying period will then have to be negotiated between you. In my experience, a period of seven to ten days is normally the outcome. Never use one offer as a 'pistol' to secure another.

At some stage between the final interview and the letter of appointment, or even after an offer is made 'subject to satisfactory references', the company may ask you two things:

1 Permission to approach previous employers.
2 For you to supply references.

The former always happens (so that the employer can check facts) but the latter is often disregarded in the case of more senior posts. Consider for a moment the real value of a reference. Here is a document, written by a selected author, which can only state good qualities (selection of author and the laws of libel would preclude anything detrimental) of the subject, and the reasons why the subject should succeed in an unknown job. Is it important? Some companies, associations and institutes and most State organizations consider it so. While this view prevails then, certainly tee-up, say, three or four highly placed personalities to write a few hundred words extolling your virtues and have them photocopied to supply any request upon demand.

One last thing to note after any interview is that you make a point of honouring any promises which you may have made during the interview. If the interviewer requests samples of your creative work or documentary evidence that your turnover was increased by *x* per cent over *y* years, and you agree to supply this evidence, then do so. Preferably deliver the documents to the company personally, with a covering letter, which you can use to your own sales advantage by drawing on additional points in your favour not mentioned at the interview. An important sales maxim is that 'people do not buy *products*, they only buy those items which they imagine will do the most for them.' You have got to prove that you will do more for the company than your competitors.

And so you have got the job—congratulations! The campaign approach has paid off. Once you have got the new job under your belt make sure that the problem does not arise again—unless you are in control of the situation. *Develop yourself* beyond the job you are doing by reading, studying, membership of societies and associations (their publications and meetings can be invaluable in broadening your horizons), and reorientate your thinking to 'It's the *job* that matters! without it we don't eat!' Become committed. (See Appendix B for suggestions and courses and seminars.)

CHECKLIST

1 The *aim* of subsequent interviews is to *shorten the list* and to *get the job.*
2 Re-read the checklist to the previous chapter.
3 You are about to meet the boss-man, the decision maker, and thus a new sales technique will be required.
4 Complete your research in all fields, especially personal reconnaissance.
5 Prepare a list of subjects to be clarified.
6 Anticipate questions and prepare the answers, but be ready for the 'googly'. Don't panic and don't 'flannel'.
7 Check the letter of appointment for the 'ten points' and any other agreements made at the interview. Never rely on 'understandings'.
8 Evaluate the firm offers you have received, and decide on the best job for *you.*
9 If 'delaying tactics' are required, be straightforward. But never use a firm offer as a 'pistol' to get another.
10 Have references ready—they may be needed.
11 Honour any promises made at the interview.
12 Send a written acceptance (or otherwise) of the offer.
13 Use the time between acceptance and joining to the fullest advantage.
14 Remember that you have not got the job until you receive a letter of appointment . . . so keep at the campaign until you have a number of firm offers.
15 Develop yourself beyond the parameters of the job.
16 Interviewee technique should not be taught. Experience (i.e. training) is the only school.

CHAPTER EIGHT

TAILPIECE TIPS

Other means of getting a job

We have examined the process of job hunting using the advertisement as our vehicle, mentioning along the way the use of round robins and personal contacts, culminating in our objective of getting a job. We have seen that before you can get a job you must get an interview. There are other ways of getting an interview which must not be overlooked. These are the use of:

Personnel consultancies.
Personnel agencies.
The Department of Employment.
The Officers' Association or similar organisations.

Personnel consultancies

Personnel consultancies work for a client. Such organisations, like Management Selection Limited, are specialists in advising employers on the selection of managerial and senior technical staff. Their clients range from some of the largest public companies to small private firms employing only a few people. They supply applicants for a broad cross-section of executive, managerial, technical and professional posts, and are thus able to draw on varied and extensive experience in advising each client on his particular problem.

Employers engage personnel consultants for three main reasons:

1 Because consultancies attract a far wider field of suitable applicants than they can themselves.
2 To use the consultancy's recruitment and selection expertise to reduce the chance factor in getting the right man for the right job.
3 To save the valuable (and expensive) time of their own staff, which they can keep at a minimum.

The normal practice is that the client approaches the consultancy to find him the right man for a particular post. The consultancy advises the client upon the need for the appointment (and his whole management structure if need be), draws up the job and personal specifications (subject to the client's approval), advertises the vacancy and selects a short list of candidates for final selection by the employer. No charge is made to the candidate.

While personnel consultancies maintain records of applicants the degree to which they use them varies widely from consultancy to consultancy. It is useless writing to an organisation like MSL asking them to help you get a job. You have to reply to one of their advertisements and, if you are suitable, be called for interview. You are really applying to the employer, but you will be dealing with professionals.

Personnel agencies

Personnel agencies work the other way around. They collect as many names as possible on their register, categorise them by type of job required, salary range, personality, etc., and then try to 'sell' the applicant to an employer. They offer to help most people who come to them, but obviously, they will concentrate upon those who have a great deal to offer, and who are easy to sell.

Some agencies go a stage further and offer a comprehensive advice, letter and CV writing service, coupled with an extensive mail shot to prospective employers.

Like anyone else agencies must cover their overheads and make a profit, so they have to charge the applicant a fee. This will range from a modest £10 to several hundreds (i.e. a percentage of the first year's salary you eventually obtain).

The Department of Employment

This is a State organisation, the services of which you have already paid for in your taxes, so to you it is free. All you have to do is to register at your local Social Security Office. As an executive your name will be passed to the Professional and Executive Register of the area(s) in which you wish to work. A synopsis of your qualifications and experience will be circulated to prospective employers. Any nibbles of interest will be relayed to you, and you take it from there.

Furthermore, once you have registered you are paid hard cash. So many people think it too degrading to 'draw the dole'. But I am sure that they do not realise how much money they can get each week—and tax free at that. You are *entitled* to two main benefits (as they are called):

1 Unemployment benefit for one year.
2 Earnings related supplement which starts 2 weeks after you become unemployed and continues for 6 months.

(A third benefit is claimable if your income drops below the State's minimum salary level, or when (1) and (2) above expire. Full details should be obtained from your local Social Security Office.)

Unemployment benefit

The basic rate for a man over 18 years of age is £5 per week, to which can be added various dependant allowances, i.e.:

Adult dependant (e.g. wife)	£3.10
First child (under 18)	1.55
Second child	0.65
Third child and all others	0.55

Earnings related supplement

Calculated as one third of the difference between £9 and your averaged weekly earnings over the past year (maximum averaged weekly earnings is £30).

Thus a man who has been earning £1500 (or more) would get an earnings related supplement of:

Averaged salary per week	£30
Deduct	9
	21
Divide by 3	7 per week

Let us examine a case and see what a married man, with three children in the 12–15 age group, earning £2000 a year would get by simply registering with the Social Security Office:

Basic benefit		£5.0
Allowances for:	Wife	3.10
	First child	1.65
	Second child	0.65
	Third child	0.55
Earnings related benefit		7.0 (maximum)
		17.95

To this should be added the cost of his National Insurance stamp which is franked free by the Social Security Office to a value of 88p. (If you don't register then you have to stamp your card yourself at the 3rd Class rate of 99p and even that does not give you full sickness, etc. cover.)

So you can collect nearly £19 a week—*tax free*. Register right away!

The Officers' Association

If you have ever held a commission in any of the armed forces of the Crown, then *do* register with the Officers' Association (28 Belgrave Square, SW1). This organisation is non-profit making and is run as a charity. Its task is to fit people who have registered with them into jobs. It will deal only with those who have not got a job at the time of applying. It maintains a register, and recommends applicants to employers. A vast number of companies use the services of the Officers' Association, and they place many hundreds of people every year.

No charge is made for the service, but obviously you would make a grateful donation to the charity if it succeeds in placing you.

Job hunting statistics

Now that we have covered most of the field of job hunting let us look at the effect of the campaign and techniques I have put forward for your consideration—and, I hope, your acceptance. The proof of the pudding is in the eating. The statistics given on the following page result from an analysis of the latest annual survey done on senior officers in search of a second career who have been trained at The Polytechnic of Central London's six-week Business Management Appreciation Course (part of which is 'Operation Bowler').

JOB HUNTING STATISTICS

	Replies to advertisements				Mail shots			Agencies	Totals
	Firms	Consultants	Box numbers	Total	Round robins	Friends	Total		
Letters written	70	20	15	105	60	30	90	20	215
Replies received	42	20	2	64	26	30	56	10	130
Application forms received	10	14	1	25	20	25	45	10	80
Interviews	3	7	0	10	10	24	34	8	52
Jobs offered	1	1	0	2	1	3	4	0	6

Note that the average job hunter has to write some 215 letters, will receive about 130 replies, has to complete 80 application forms, attend 50 interviews and will eventually be offered about 6 jobs. The average time taken to get a job is about 6 months.

Study the figures carefully stage by stage. The percentages of success were:

Replies to advertisements	2%
Mail shots	4·4%
(Note: personal friends 10%)	

Certainly the most profitable area is personal friends.

At least these figures will serve as an indication of the size of the campaign you have to mount, and the areas of the market which you can attack initially. You will have to adjust your tactics as you analyse your own results achieved.

Immediate action

As soon as you are out of a job it is suggested that you take immediate action in the following areas:

1 *Tell your wife immediately*. She has a right to know, and she will probably be a great help to you psychologically. She will be someone you can talk to about the problem and your plans for the future. She will help you blow off steam, and may well have many constructive ideas about what you can do in the future and will certainly take some of the worry away from you. She may even take a job to help with the finances. One wife I know did just this. She became a cosmetics sales lady but only on a temporary basis until her husband got fixed up. When this happened, about six months later, she found that she enjoyed the work so much (so different from the daily household routine), and her commission on sales was so good, that she and her husband decided that she would stay on with the company. Their joint income exceeded their wildest expectations, and they were able to enjoy many luxuries which previously they would never have been able to afford. Moral, with tongue in cheek, 'put your wife out to work'!

2 *Register with the Department of Employment* and collect a reasonable tax-free salary every week. The Professional and Executive Register may even supply you with a job.

3 *Register with every possible job finding agency*, preferably those which do not charge the applicant a fee. However, don't discard those that do completely out of hand. See what they have to offer, and judge their worth in your case. Having read this book, I reckon that you should be able to do their job better than they can, because you will be selling you—personally—and this counts highly with employers.

NB

4 *Prepare your marketing campaign.* Allocate your budget, marshal the facts, prepare your personal record sheet, compile your CV, draft your master letter, research the market, decide your target areas and go to work.

5 *Order the* Daily Telegraph, The Times, *the* Financial Times *and the* Sunday Times. Study the advertisements to get a feel of the market. Read all the company annual reports, and study the City pages. Analyse advertisements, and go for those jobs where you have a seven out of ten chance of getting an interview. Look at the possibility of several part time jobs as opposed to a full time one. This could be more suitable for you. In fact you would be building up your 'own business', and all your eggs would not be in one basket.

6 *Immediately start travelling first class.* It is in the first class carriages that you will meet the people who matter, and whose help and advice it is you seek.

7 *Go on holiday.* I advise you to go on the most expensive holiday you can afford for the same reasons as in (6) above.

8 *Start your marketing campaign* as soon as you get back. Open all the stops and don't miss a trick. Get into the mental state which reacts quickly and positively to any potential opening, almost to the state of: when you go into a public loo and see scrawled on the wall 'Kilroy was here', whip out your magic marker and write 'And here's his CV.'

9 *Keep going until you get a number of firm offers.* Then sit back and decide which job is the best for you.

10 *Keep your mind alert and in good shape.* Maintain campaign records, an efficient personal filing system and keep reading

avidly. Consider enrolling on short or one-day management courses at business schools, polytechnics or technical colleges. Write off for prospectuses, and select those courses which will stand you in good stead in your career. A list of some suggested courses is given at Appendix B.

So that's it—that's about all I can tell you. All I can do is to wish you the very best of luck in your campaign (I hope you enjoy becoming a professional interviewee) and suggest that, now you have finished this book, READ IT AGAIN, AND AGAIN, AND AGAIN.

APPENDIX A

SOME EXAMPLES OF A CURRICULUM VITAE

Junior executive

JOHN THOMAS ARMITAGE

Born: 13.4.4– (26). Married. One child aged 3.
Address: 15 Shark Square, London, S.W.1. (01) 580–4346.

EDUCATION AND QUALIFICATIONS

Secondary Modern School. 5 'O' levels (195– to 195–)
Mathematics, English, History, Chemistry and Physics.
I am currently studying for the H.N.C. in Business Studies at Westminster Technical College, and have completed two years of the three-year evening course.

CAREER

On leaving school (age 16) I joined the Monastry Insurance Company as a clerk where I served for two years in the Accounts Office. In 196– I joined Snodgrass and Co. Ltd. as a sales correspondent on the export side of the business. In 196– I was appointed as the Surrey representative of the company. To widen my horizons I joined Enfield Electronics Ltd. as the representative responsible for London and the South East of England. I have been with this company for the past four years.

EXPERIENCE

Clerical The years I spent as an Accounts Clerk have proved most valuable because I received a sound grounding in the fundamentals of accountancy, office clerical procedures and the principles of good office administration. My time as a sales correspondent taught me how to express myself clearly and concisely in writing. I have also had experience of maintaining sales records, an insight into credit control, and sales and marketing budgeting.

Sales With Snodgrass and Co. Ltd. I was concerned with selling (by remote control) a range of pharmaceutical products. It was in this highly competitive market that I discovered I could sell, not only to export agents, overseas buyers, but also face-to-face with representatives of foreign companies. When I took over the Surrey territory I found potential in unexplored outlets, so that I was selling to medical practitioners as well as to the retail trade. In four years I had increased the sales of my territory by 400% to a current figure of £*x* p.a.

The consumer durable field was entirely new to me when I joined Enfield Electronics, but an excellent induction course run by the company, and a period 'under instruction' in the field soon gave me the knowledge necessary to take over the London and S.E. area. During my time with Enfield Electronics I have expanded my company's trade in the South East from £*a* to £*b* p.a. and have opened up over 1200 new accounts.

GENERAL

I am a keen gardener and family man. My hobbies include: debating, reading and football. My wife and I are renting our flat in London, but we are buying a small cottage in Norfolk which we are modernising ourselves.

AIM

Financial stringency has forced my company to reduce its sales force by 50%, together with a large number of administrative personnel. Thus I am seeking a sales or marketing appointment where my knowledge of outlets and territories will be valuable.

Middle executive

JOHN THOMAS ARMITAGE

Born: 13.4.2– (50). Widower. Three adult children.
Address: 15, Shark Square, London, S.W.1. (01) 580–4346.

EDUCATION AND QUALIFICATIONS

Glasgow Academy (192– to 193–). Scottish Senior Leaving Certificate (English, Mathematics, History, French, German.)
Member of the Institute of Office Management, Associate Member of the British Institute of Management.

CAREER

On leaving school (age 18) I was very keen to enter the agricultural industry, so took a job as a trainee manager in the Highlands. On the outbreak of war, I joined the Royal Air Force and trained as a navigator in South Africa. I flew with bombers in the Middle East and the Balkans and was demobilised as a Flight Lieutenant in 1946. In 194– I emigrated to Kenya and took up farming (cattle and corn). This profitable venture ended with Kenyan independence. I returned to the UK in 195–. Since then I have worked as a salesman, school bursar, and am currently the Sales Office Manager of Enfield Electronics Ltd.

EXPERIENCE

Farm Management For nearly ten years I ran my own farm in Kenya. As this was a private venture, I was personally responsible (with my own capital at stake), for the profitability of the operation. I was my own personnel officer, corporate planner, accountant, buyer, salesman and 'managing director'. My wife and I started from nothing (even building our house) and developed the farm to *x* head of cattle and *y* acres under cultivation, giving a turnover of £*x* p.a. My farm was compulsorily purchased in 195– when I returned to the UK.

Sales For 2 years (195– to 195–) I was the Anglian representative for a fertiliser manufacturer (Jones & Black Ltd.) selling the full range of products to farmers.

Although I increased my area turnover by 20% in this period I felt that the remuneration was not commensurate with my contribution to the profitability of the company.

Bursarship For the next four years I was the Bursar of Greyfriars Preparatory School, near Colchester. My wife took on the responsibilities of Matron, and I dealt with all administration (non-academic) of the School. My duties included domestic budgeting, maintenance of the house and grounds, and the supply of all teaching materials. I was responsible for the recruitment and selection of all non-academic staff and managing the whole establishment. It was a '24 hour-a-day' job which I enjoyed very much, and I was sorry when the school closed down in 196–.

Office Management My administrative experience stood me in good stead, and I secured the appointment of Sales Office Manager of Enfield Electronics Ltd. My responsibilities cover the coordination of the activities of the four sections of the Sales Department. (Enquiries/orders processing, sales records, credit control and despatch.) I have a staff of 104 people, and am responsible to the General Sales Manager for the whole administration of both the Sales and Marketing Departments. Owing to financial constraints within the company, my appointment is being abolished within the next three months.

GENERAL

I am an enthusiatic member of the local operatic society, a keen horticulturist, and my hobbies include music, reading and ornithology. My aim is to secure a worthwhile and progressive administrative post for the next 15 years.

Senior executive

JOHN THOMAS ARMITAGE

Born: 13.4.2– (48). Married, one adult child at University.
Address: 15 Shark Square, London, S.W.1. (01) 580–4346.

EDUCATION AND QUALIFICATIONS

Grammar School (Blankaster) 193– to 193–. Oxford School Certificate, 7 subjects 3 credits; Higher School Certificate Mathematics, Physics, Chemistry, English. *Graduate of*: London University B.Sc. (Eng.) at age 25; *London Business School* (Advanced Management) at age 36, Polytechnic of Central London, *School of Management Studies*, Industrial Marketing Course (196–).
Elected M.B.I.M. (196–), Fellow 196–. M.I.Mech.E.

CAREER

Joined the Army from school (age 18). Commissioned into the Royal Garhwal Rifles from Indian Military Academy. Served in North Africa, Italy and N.W. Europe. Demobilized with the rank of Major (*MC*). After graduating, I worked for a number of light engineering companies gaining rapid promotion to Works Engineer. I continued my studies on evening courses thus gaining knowledge of all aspects of management, the techniques of which I was able to practise and improve in my work. The appointment to Works Manager of XYZ Co. Ltd. led (2 years later) to a seat on the Board of one of its subsidiaries. Subsequently, I was appointed to main board as Managing Director.

EXPERIENCE

Engineering Four years (194– to 195–) with Bloggs & Co. Ltd, castings engineers, starting as a stress engineer, rising to Project Leader. In charge of Ministry contracts, reporting to progress meetings with Company Directors. In 195– moved to Blankson Ltd. on promotion to Assistant Works Manager, and two years later was appointed Works Engineer, responsible for the total production of the factory. In 195– I joined XYZ Co. Ltd. as Works Manager with responsibility for the planning and complete production of three factories. Gained rapid promotion based on results, so that in 196– I was appointed to the Board as Production Director.

Higher Management The appointment of Production Director allowed me to introduce new techniques of control which resulted in a 25% increase in production output. Three years later I was made Managing Director of the Consumer Goods Division (on Group reorganisation), responsible to the Group Chairman for international direction of the company's activities and the profitability of my division. Present profit £2.5 m. p.a.

GENERAL

I have travelled extensively throughout the world, but mainly in Europe, the USA and Canada. I am a keen golfer (7) and photographer. I am a member of the XXXX Society, and take an active interest in the affairs of the community in which I live.

AIM

Owing to the takeover of my company by the CED Group, and the consequent reorganisation of the whole management structure, I am seeking further challenging responsibilities for the next 15 years. My wife and I own our house in London, but are willing to go anywhere.

Overseas Civil Servant

JOHN THOMAS ARMITAGE

Born: 13.4.2– (48). Bachelor.
Address: 15, Shark Square, London, SW.1. (01) 580–4346.

EDUCATION AND QUALIFICATIONS

Public School (Blankaster) 193– to 194–. Oxford School Certificate (exemption London Matriculation). London University: 1 year course in Arabic (age 19). Colonial Administrative Course (age 25).

H.M. OVERSEAS CIVIL SERVICE CAREER

After 4 years' war service in the Royal Navy (Lt. RNVR) I joined H.M. Overseas Civil Service. Served in Palestine (2 years), Kenya (3 years), and Tanzania (18 years). I have held the posts of Staff Officer, Executive Officer, Principal Assistant Secretary, District Commissioner and Assistant Administrator.

EXPERIENCE

Planning For the past 5 years I have had specialised experience assisting the Minister, and various committees, on the formulation of administrative policy, based on the views of experts in other disciplines. I was responsible for the drafting of Cabinet Papers, and the provision of administrative and secretarial services to Councils and other organisations. In Ministry Planning Units I was responsible for the collection and collation of data for economic, staff and corporate planning procedures. As Chairman of three committees, I was involved in national communications, siting and building of airports, and tourism. I have also been concerned with the formulation and execution of education plans at Central and Local Government levels.

Management As District Commissioner, I managed departments totalling 350 people. I was responsible for the recruitment and training of staff. As the Ministry O & M Officer I was responsible for the office systems, discipline and records of the Ministry with an establishment of 5000.

Budgeting Experience as a Sub-Accountant in District Revenue Offices, District Commissioner for the local government treasury. Duties included: estimating, revenue control, budgeting, (£*x* p.a.) and final financial statements.

GENERAL

I have knowledge of the Middle East and East Africa, from political, economic, cultural and geographic viewpoints. I have travelled widely in Europe, the Far East and Australasia. My experience includes the management of staff of all grades and many nationalities. I speak fluent Swahili, and my interests are squash, riding, sailing and reading. As I have only recently returned to UK I am renting a flat in London. My aim is to start a new career and I am willing to move to any part of the world.

Note that all CVs should be typed on one sheet of A4 paper.

APPENDIX B

SOME SUITABLE SHORT COURSES AND SEMINARS

This list is by no means exhaustive. Its purpose is to show you the types of courses available to you at management studies centres so that you will be encouraged to make further enquiries. Such courses are heavily subsidised and cost in the region of £10 per day.

One-day courses

Discounted cash flow
Capital investments decisions are among the most critical that are made by management. This one-day seminar is designed to provide managers with an understanding of the use of this technique for appraising capital investment projects.

Balance sheet interpretation
Senior managers, personal assistants, secretaries, etc., should be able to interpret and understand the published accounts of companies. This one-day seminar explains in plain, non-technical terms how a balance sheet is drawn up, what information it contains and what general facts can be interpreted from the analysis.

Forecasting by computer
This one-day course indicates the various forecasting techniques and indicates their use on a computer terminal.

Critical path analysis; appreciation
Critical path analysis has become an accepted tool for the planning and control of projects (in any sphere). This one-day course gives members an overall appreciation of the technique and its application.

Two- and three-day courses

Inventory regulation by grid
A two-day seminar and workshop designed to study a major

advance in this complex management area. It aims to ensure absolute management control and coordination in manufacturing operations of any complexity and to eliminate panic situations. Manufactured, subcontracted and purchased items are catered for.

Bidding strategy
A three-day seminar to provide an approach to the determination of bidding policy and the optimisation of bids. The relevance of bidding theory and recent research to the practical problems of estimating, pricing and bidding is considered. The seminar will interest senior staff responsible for the formulation of bidding policy and the submission of bids in contracting industries such as electronics, construction, shipbuilding, etc.

Elementary numerical methods for management
An unashamedly basic course of management mathematics with an emphasis on graphical methods and statistics. Wide experience of management teaching has shown that otherwise experienced and qualified managers often feel the need to brush up their knowledge of the relevant basic maths. This three-day course aims to meet this need.

One-week courses

Financial aspects of management
This one-week course is designed to introduce managers, trades union officials and others interested in interpreting financial statements produced by organisations to the accounting and finance function of present day industrial and commercial concerns. The course is particularly for those with no previous knowledge of these aspects, and will cover basic concepts of accounting, the nature of funds, deployment of financial resources and evaluation of financial reports, etc.

The job of the personnel officer
The aim of this one-week course is to provide an introduction to personnel work, and to the role and function of the personnel officer in an organisation. Different aspects of personnel work are introduced, thus providing an overview of the subject. It is most suitable for assistant personnel officers, for those who have been recently appointed to personnel posts, or for those

who require rapid familiarisation with the scope of personnel work as part of their general management training.

Decisions in marketing (the Bayesian approach)
A one-week course for marketing executives, brand and product managers, agency account executives, etc., designed to enable members to understand and use valuable and as yet under-exploited techniques for decision-making in marketing. The syllabus includes how to deal rationally with problems involving risk and uncertainty, how to achieve consistency in corporate decision-making and risk-taking, and how to evaluate marketing information. Emphasis is given to the practicalities of marketing decision problems, and the mathematics are not at a difficult level.

Work study appreciation
A one-week course to give managers the information they need about method study, work measurement, value analysis, critical path analysis and computers, to enable them to make the best of specialist management services.

Organisation and method appreciation
Organisation and Method studies are better implemented if managers understand the objectives and procedures of the management services specialist. This one-week course provides for managers in industry, commerce and administration, the understanding they need to cooperate with O & M practitioners, particularly in the field of clerical work measurement, productivity reporting and productivity bargaining.

Critical path
Critical path analysis, PERT and activity-on-node are examples of the range of planning and control techniques based on network analysis. This one-week course enables its members to draw and analyse networks manually or by computer.

(Reprinted by kind permission of The School of Management Studies, The Polytechnic of Central London, 35 Marylebone Road, London NW1.)

APPENDIX C

ESPECIALLY FOR SERVICE OFFICERS

Although this Appendix has been written specifically for officers of the armed forces who are seeking a new career in industry, much of it could apply equally to Warrant Officers and senior Non-Commissioned Officers with the same aim in mind. Everything which has been said in this book is applicable to you, but there are specific areas which need elaborating for your particular case.

Fundamentally, you are faced with the old image of the service officer (Colonel Blimp) which still persists in many boardrooms, and the memories the senior managers have of the officers under whom they served during the Second World War. By and large, the bosses in industry do not know how radically the Services have changed over the last ten years.

Let us look at these specific areas where you need more advice.

Contribution factor

During the past *x* years your contribution factor has been measured in terms of your ability to do a wide variety of administrative jobs well. Although you have been concerned with administrating funds you have not been involved in *making a profit*. That is what business is all about! The major factor of a serviceman's reorientation to a civilian career is to understand that everything, but everything, in the business world is geared to this end. The £ sterling, like Calais and Mary Tudor, must be engraved on your heart!

What is available?

The Service officer is highly trained and self-reliant. This is what industry requires in its management team. Why? because a highly trained man must be a mentally disciplined man, but he must not be inhibited. He must be capable of assimilating facts and know-how quickly, retaining them and putting them to good use. A manager is a leader who can get the most out of people, know his job, think clearly and plan concisely.

The Service officer has a great deal to offer but he must be enthusiastic, ready to take his coat off and to accept people at their 'profitability value'. The following give some idea of what is available to him in the wide world of commerce and industry:

BIG BUSINESS The bulk of commerce and industry is engaged in buying something, doing something with it and selling it at a profit. (Manufacturing, marketing, selling administrating, trading, agencies of all types.)

SPECIALIST ORGANISATIONS These supply a service to Big Business. Consultancies, engineering of all types, management, personnel, advertising, public relations, etc., journalism, printing. You name it, there must be a consultancy for it.

'PERIPHERY' ORGANISATIONS These are not directly concerned with Big Business, but serve sections of industry, the State, the community or groups of businesses. (Societies, institutions, schools, colleges, universities, trusts, commissions, trade associations, charities, civil service.)

Business appreciation courses

The Ministry of Defence in collaboration with the Department of Employment has organised special Business Appreciation Courses at certain polytechnics and technical colleges specially designed for officers of the armed forces (and those of the Foreign and Commonwealth Department and the Overseas Civil Service). These courses explain the complex business world, and translate service knowledge and experience into civilian management techniques. Application for attendance upon such courses should be made through Service channels.

Application forms

As these forms are designed for the use of civilian applicants there is seldom sufficient space for you to deal with your career in the services in the section provided. I suggest that you write 'see CV attached' in this space, and send your CV with the form when you return it.

Retired pay and pensions

It is, unfortunately, still a fact that a few companies regard servicemen as a source of cheap labour and try to lower the true rate for the job by saying: '. . . but, as you have a substantial income from your pension . . . you will no doubt work for a smaller salary'. This, of course, is inquitous because such companies do not take into account a civilian's private income when taking him on. You have already paid for your pension—it was part of your pay! You should, in such a situation, consider very hard if you want to work for such a parsimonious organisation.

The curriculum vitae

Examples of a service officer's and a Senior NCO's CV are given on the next two pages. Important points to note are:

> EDUCATION PARAGRAPH Make this paragraph show that your education has never stopped. Pause to think how many *years* of courses you have received during your service and what this would constitute in terms of capital investment in you.
>
> CAREER PARAGRAPH Keep this as short as possible as this is not a selling paragraph. You cannot sell the fact that you have been a serviceman for *x* years, but you can sell the valuable experience you have gained during those years. This is what you do in the next paragraph.
>
> EXPERIENCE PARAGRAPH This is the one that matters. No militarese or jargon please. Never use service abbreviations (e.g. GSO 3 (Int), or DADOS, or DAA & QMG) because they will not be understood. Every sub-paragraph must have an 'end product'—what did you achieve?

Never write a chronological list of appointments.

Service officer

JOHN THOMAS ARMITAGE

Born: 13.4.2– (48). Married, 3 children (1 at school).
Address: 15 Shark Square, London S.W.1. (01) 580–4346.

EDUCATION AND QUALIFICATIONS

Public School (Blankaster) 193– to 193–. Oxford University School Certificate 6 credits. Entered Sandhurst (age 19) by competitive examination.
Commissioned to Royal Artillery 193–.
Graduate of: Army Staff College (age 29), Joint Services Staff College (age 33), NATO Defence College (age 36).
Russian Interpretership (2nd Class) London University 196–.
Elected *A.M.B.I.M.* (197–). *C.I.S.* passed 2 (of 3) parts of Finals (196– and 196–), writing last part 197–.

CAREER IN THE ARMY

33 years from 2nd Lt. to Colonel (CBE, MC) to March 197–.
During the past 10 years I have held the following senior appointments:

196– to 197– Commandant of Army School (1500 soldiers and civilians).
196– to 196– Military Attaché in Athens.
196– to 196– Senior Staff Officer, NATO HQ Europe.
196– to 196– Command of a Field Regt. (800 officers and soldiers).

EXPERIENCE

Training As an instructor at the School of Infantry I was responsible for planning, administering and lecturing on courses which were tailored to meet the needs of junior and senior officers, and which dealt with all matters of staff management. Later, as Commandant of an Army School, I organised the training and administration of 1500 young men.

Sales and P.R. For three years I negotiated with Greek Civil and Military authorities on behalf of British Armament Manufacturers. Personally organised four demonstrations of arms to selected Greek audiences (1200) and two demonstrations of communications equipment valued at £4 m.
Contracts worth £$1\frac{1}{2}$ m. came to fruition during this period and a further £2 m. were pending.

Civilian Administration In my last appointment my civilian staff consisted of some 200 instructors, and a further 200 administrative staff giving me experience of handling civilian staffs of highly diverse grades; and as a member of the Whitley Council of negotiating with trades union representatives.

Forward Planning and Committee Work For three years (196– to 196–) as a Senior Staff Officer at NATO Headquarters, I was responsible for preparing argued papers and briefs for consideration by the Chiefs of Staff, on forward planning, operational and logistic requirements, organisation and international cooperation: and served on three committees—one as Chairman with members of five nationalities (weekly meetings).

General I have travelled 10,000 miles throughout Europe, and lived for more than 2 years in India–Burma–Malaysia–Austria–Germany and France. I have visited the USA and Canada. Consequently, I have had the opportunity of studying the thinking and psychology of many different nationalities. I speak fluent Russian and French; I am a keen photographer; and have published three books (both in this country and overseas). I play most outdoor sports (represented the Army at Rugby 193–/3–).

AIM

I am seeking challenging responsibilities for the next *y* years. My wife and I own our house in London, but we are willing to go anywhere. My aim is to make a new career in civilian life.

Flight Sergeant, R.A.F.

JOHN THOMAS ARMITAGE

Leaving the Royal Air Force (as a Flight Sergeant) after a 22-year enagagement in September 197– at the age of 4–.
Born: 13.4.2–. Married with three dependent children.
Address: 15 Shark Square, London, S.W.1. (01) 580–4346.

EDUCATION AND QUALIFICATIONS

Grammar School (Blankford) until joining the R.A.F. at age 16. Qualified as a Radar Operator after a 3 months' course, and over the next 4 years passed G.C.E. at 'O' level in Mathematics, English, Geography, and History. Trained typist and office administrator. Passed Senior NCO's Management Course at age 37.

CAREER IN THE ROYAL AIR FORCE

After 4 years as a Radar Operator, I transferred to the secretarial side of the R.A.F. I qualified as a typist and later attended 3 administrative courses. I have held the rank of Flight Sergeant for the last ten years.

EXPERIENCE

Secretarial After training in general clerical duties I was appointed to the rank of Corporal in charge of the Registry at an Aircrew Selection Centre. For 4 years I was responsible for the collection, registration and dissemination of all mail arriving at the Centre. The day-to-day operation of the Centre's filing system was also my responsibility. It was during this period that I gained an efficient grounding in office and clerical procedures.

Training On promotion to Sergeant (196–) I was selected as an instructor at an R.A.F. clerical school teaching: typing, filing, office systems and administration. Courses consisted of some 40 Corporals and Sergeants. Two and a half years later I was appointed to a station employing 1500 men, where I was responsible for the coordination of all 'on-the-job' training. It was at this time that I was promoted Flight Sergeant.

Office Administration I spent two periods of two years as NCO in charge of a Station Orderly Room in which appointment I was responsible for the clerical efficiency of the headquarters. This involved PA duties to the Commanding Officer (Group Captain), selection of clerical personnel, O & M administering pay and all records and the coordination of all the adminstrative activities of the station.

GENERAL

I have travelled extensively in Europe, and have lived more than 2 years in Germany, Cyprus, Aden and Malaysia. My staffs have included airmen and airwomen, and civilians of many nationalities. I am a keen motorist and caravaner, and play most outdoor sports. I am a qualified football referee.

AIM

I am seeking further responsibilities for the next 25 years. My wife and I are willing to go anywhere in the United Kingdom.

APPENDIX D

A LETTER OF APPLICATION

Follow the principles already detailed in Chapter 5. However, the following example may help you in drafting your letter:
(*No name, etc. at the top of the letter*)

15, Shark Square,
London, S.W.1
(01) 580–4346
6th September, 197–

The Group Personnel Director,
The ABC Group of Companies Ltd
ABC House,
London, W1P3FG

Dear Sir,

STAFF MANAGER: CROYDON ACCESSORIES LTD

I have read your advertisement in today's *Daily Telegraph* for a Staff Manager at your Croydon factory, and request to be considered as a candidate.

I shall be leaving the Army normally (with the rank of Colonel) in about eight weeks' time after 32 years' service. I am at present attending an intensive business training course at . . . which has been specially designed to meet the requirements of officers leaving the services, with the aim of fitting them for appointments in industrial and commercial management.

(Then should follow details of your experience which covers as many of the specified points in the advertisement as possible.)

I have practised the principles of management for the past *x* years as a staff officer in the following appointments, all of which have demanded organising and staff management ability:

(a) (rank)
(b) (rank)

(A few sentences about each extracted from your CV and amplified in relation to the job)

In (b) above I was personally responsible for the administration and terms of service of some . . . civilian employees of various grades.

I can attend an interview at any time to suit you.

Yours faithfully,

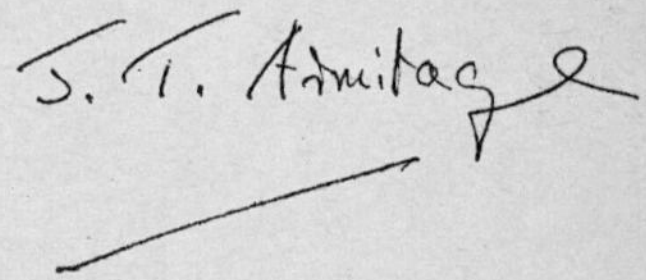

J. T. Armitage

(*No rank*)

(*Do not attach your CV to this letter*)

OTHER TITLES IN THE SAME SERIES

A Business of Your Own

LESLEY BERNSTEIN AND SYLVIA PASKIN

Every day thousands of people dream about setting up a business of their own. The attractions of independence, of being 'your own boss', are strong. Many eventually take that step and never regret it. Here are true stories of people who have set up on their own – what made them take that step, their problems, their successes, their methods and mistakes. Written by two professional journalists, this is an excellent way of seeing how to do it, by reading how others have 'made the break'.

A PAPERBACK ORIGINAL
$7\frac{1}{2}''\times4\frac{1}{2}''$ (191 mm × 114 mm)   112 pp
ISBN 0 220 66832 9 **50p**

Simon Elliott's Quick Guides to Speaking in Public

SIMON ELLIOTT

From best man to company chairman, from a farewell party to television interview – hardly anyone escapes having to speak to a gathering of people a few times in their lives. And the more successful a person is in his career or hobby, the more he has to speak in public. This book is written by a person (Simon Elliott is his pen name) who is much sought after as an after dinner speaker, who has been successfully speaking in public since school debates, and through courts and parliament. His book is an excellent guide to what to say, when to say it, and how to say it.

A PAPERBACK ORIGINAL
$7\frac{1}{2}''\times4\frac{1}{2}''$ (191 mm × 114 mm)   112 pp
ISBN 0 220 66831 0 **50p**

SOME TITLES PUBLISHED IN HARDBACK BY BUSINESS BOOKS LIMITED

no. of copies	international standard book number	price	title
——	0 220 66877 9	£6·30	**The business and professional man's lawyer** *Mitchell*
——	0 220 66875 2	£3·50	**The businessman's guide to letter-writing and to the law on letters** *Mitchell*
——	0 220 66799 3	£3·75	**Enjoying a profitable business** *Hazel and Reid*
——	0 220 69859 7	£2·25	**Etiquette for the businessman** *Bosticco*
——	0 220 79891 5	£3·50	**Finance for the non-accountant** *Rockley*
——	0 220 79865 6	£3·25	**Fund raising techniques** *Phillips*
——	0 220 79419 7	£3·75	**Graphics ad lib** *Hinwood*
——	0 220 79866 4	£2·75	**Industrial intelligence and espionage** *Slee Smith*
——	0 220 79946 6	£4·20	**Management systems for the hotel, catering and allied industries** *Fearn*
——	0 220 99258 4	£2·50	**The measurement of capital employed** *Pierce*
——	0 220 99222 3	£3·25	**Spending advertising money** *Broadbent*
——	0 220 99261 4	£4·75	**Successful project management** *Taylor & Watling*
——	0 220 79932 6	£2·10	**Top secretary** *Bosticco*

ORDER FORM

ORDER FROM YOUR BOOKSELLER

Simply mark the books you require on this form and give it to your normal bookseller

All enquiries to:

BUSINESS BOOKS LIMITED
MERCURY HOUSE
WATERLOO ROAD
LONDON SE1 8UL

Telephone: 01-928 3388

CUSTOMER'S NAME AND ADDRESS

DATE: ORDER NO.